Praise for *Dance Your Dance*

"Laurieann Gibson is what my late friend James Ingram and I call a CREATE. That special human being who is born of pure openness, curiosity, and daring that leads them to explore untreaded paths that light the world. I have long admired her genius as a creative director and choreographer. This book is yet another chapter in her journey of inspired generosity."

—DEBBIE ALLEN
EMMY AWARD–WINNING CHOREOGRAPHER,
ACTRESS, TV DIRECTOR, AND TV PRODUCER

"Every artist needs a coach. Laurieann has been my coach, and there's nobody better. Laurieann has brought out the best in me. She's a true visionary and has impacted culture in a revolutionary way. This book will keep you inspired on your road to fulfilling your dream."

—SEAN "DIDDY" COMBS
CHAIRMAN AND CEO, COMBS ENTERPRISES;
MULTI-PLATINUM-SELLING AND GRAMMY AWARD–WINNING RAPPER,
SINGER, SONGWRITER, RECORD PRODUCER, AND RECORD EXECUTIVE

"Laurieann Gibson: this magnetic, magical artist and creative genius changed my life when I started to work with her. I felt like I was growing and groomed to be the artist God intended me to be. Laurie's passion, spirit, and respect for the arts are unmatched in her expression of them. She brings out the light in any star she's worked with, and I am truly blessed to have been trained, uplifted, and inspired.

"Laurie, you are one of my sheroes. I wouldn't be the artist I am today if our paths didn't cross. I am so excited for your book and all that is yet to come to you. You deserve it all."

—BRANDEE NORWOOD
SINGER, SONGWRITER, AND ACTRESS

"Laurieann is like thunder, lightning, and energy all wrapped up in the human form. The moment she steps into the room, it is electrified, and whoever is in that room can never question the energy shift! As a performer, she always dared me to dream bigger and be bolder, more expansive, more curious. She pushed me to the edges of my comfort zone. These are some of the many things I've learned from her and that I continue to apply to my artistry today. Everything is purposeful; the purpose feeds the movement, the movement tells a story, the story is the art.

"I am honored to know her and excited that she has chosen to open up and share this powerful knowledge of how to dance your dance, move to your own rhythm, and make your mark on the world!"

—ALICIA KEYS
MULTI-PLATINUM-SELLING AND GRAMMY AWARD–WINNING SINGER, SONGWRITER, RECORDING ARTIST, ACTRESS, AND PHILANTHROPIST

"My dear friend and sister Laurieann Gibson exemplifies a life lived on assignment. Laurieann's sense and awareness of purpose is pungent, contagious, and inspiring. In the many years I have known Laurieann, there have been very few people's lives that have encouraged and impressed me like my sister's. Her daringness to magnanimously dream, her determination to press through—spiritually, psychologically, and physically—in order to fulfill that dream, and the lessons that she has gleaned along the way in dancing it all out will most certainly inspire you to dance your dance."

—PASTOR DUSTIN HAWKINS
PLACE FOR LIFE, SAN ANTONIO, TEXAS

DANCE
your
DANCE

8 STEPS TO UNLEASH YOUR PASSION
AND LIVE YOUR DREAM

LAURIEANN GIBSON

WITH MARK DAGOSTINO

W Publishing Group

An Imprint of Thomas Nelson

Dance Your Dance

© 2021 Laurieann Gibson

Published in Nashville, Tennessee, by W Publishing, an imprint of Thomas Nelson.

Thomas Nelson titles may be purchased in bulk for educational, business, fundraising, or sales promotional use. For information, please e-mail SpecialMarkets@ThomasNelson.com.

Unless otherwise noted, Scripture quotations are taken from the New King James Version®. Copyright © 1982 by Thomas Nelson. Used by permission. All rights reserved.

Scripture quotations marked KJV are taken from the King James Version. Public domain.

ISBN 978-0-7852-3434-0 (audiobook)
ISBN 978-0-7852-3431-9 (eBook)
ISBN 978-0-7852-3430-2 (HC)

Library of Congress Catalog-in-Publication Data
Library of Congress Control Number: 2020946990

Printed in the United States of America
21 22 23 24 25 LSC 10 9 8 7 6 5 4 3 2 1

To my father,
Lauriston George Gibson,
1940–2008.
Daddy, I miss you. Thanks for
keeping the cardboard box for me.

And to all the dreamers of the world:
Be steadfast. Never give up. It's
your right. It belongs to you!

Contents

Prelude

*L*isten up!

Come closer now.

Gather 'round. It's all right.

It's quiet now. Before the music starts. The crowd is hushed and we're all backstage, behind the curtain, waiting for our moment. Waiting for the beginning. Waiting to share our gifts. Waiting to shine.

It's exciting, right? You can feel the energy.

It's here where I want to speak your dream.

Go on. Dig deep. I want you to remember, to see, to hear, to *feel* the dream that is deep inside you.

I want to speak to the dreams that you had way back when you were little, before the world got to you; to the dreams that might have been washed away; to the ones they said you couldn't have because you don't *look like* or *move like* or *sound like* or *talk like* or *come from the place* that somebody else does.

I want to speak to the dreamer in you: the dancer, the artist, the singer, the writer, the visionary, the mover, the shaker, the thinker. The part of you that might be buried, lost but not forgotten. That little piece inside of you that knows your joy and makes you smile at the very thought of it; that quiet voice inside that shakes you up when you listen to it; that voice that puts a kick-snare boom-*kack* rhythm in your heart.

The thing that makes you feel *alive*.

The passion that takes hold of you just by thinking about it.

And when you're in it, when you're *feeling* it, you don't think about anything else. You *can't* think about anything else. It brings you to a place where you forget about your worries; where there are no deadlines, no bills, no fights, no pain, no past, no future. Where you're deep in your element, loving life, feeling easy and free.

Yeah, you know what I'm talkin' about. And even if you don't right now, that's okay. We're gonna find it.

Close your eyes for a moment. Take a deep breath. *Remember.*

That feeling, that dream, that creative *thing* down deep in your soul: that is your *truth.* And your truth in itself should allow you to be confident about who you are—because it was put there by God. That truth is yours, and yours alone, and it is not meant to be ignored. That passion you feel or that you once felt; that creative spark; that thing that brings you joy or that brought you joy when you were young and innocent and open—it's meant to be listened to! It's meant to be taken seriously. It's meant to be enjoyed to the fullest.

I know there are people around you who've said, "You can't," "You won't," "You *what*?" "No way," "You're not good enough," or "Nu-uh, child, you're not up to the task," because you don't look or act like whatever it is they already know; because you're nothing like whoever it is that *they* think of as the dancer, the writer, the poet, the singer, the creative spirit that inspires *them.*

They. Are. Wrong.

I promise you.

God wants you to know that you don't have to look a certain way or act a certain way or sing a certain way or move a certain way in order to live out the joy of your gift. Because everyone's gift is different, and everyone's view is different too.

They might tell you that somebody else is the example you need to follow.

They might put others on a pedestal as a way to hold you down.

They might do all they can to make you think that what makes you unique isn't enough because somebody else came first and what they're doing is bigger and better and more fabulous than anything you could ever be.

All of that is a lie.

We have to identify and move past our Dreamkillers—the doors that close, the circumstances that feel like a block or a setback, the naysayers, the expressions of the oppressive mindsets of people living in fear—if we want to keep going. And we *can* move past them, through them, around them; we can even help people who are Dreamkillers to grow too! But it has to start with you.

The truth of who you are, of who you can be, of who you always were is more brilliant than the lie could ever be. *Finding* your truth, *believing* in your truth, *unleashing* your truth is what will set you free—and send you soaring into the beautiful process of *becoming*.

Becoming who you are.

Becoming who you are meant to be.

Becoming who God always wanted you to be.

It is then that you go from becoming to actually *being*; unapologetically being, no matter what comes against you, no matter what sort of Dreamkillers you face, no matter what stage you think you're in or what stage you want to be on. The painter, the architect, the athlete, the entrepreneur, the visionary—being *that* is the goal and the gift, right now, from this moment forward. Not when you're finally doing it, but when you're in the garage, in the basement, in your bedroom, in your studio, in the locker room, at your desk, at your day job, at school, wherever you are—because *being* is always and forever your truth.

And if that sounds like a lot to take in, don't worry. I'm here to help you.

This is the reason that God led me from my start as a dancer into the process of *becoming* and *being* the choreographer, the creative director, the creative visionary and teacher I am. It's the reason God insisted it was time for me to write this book!

By showing you the steps on the road I've taken, and the steps in the dance we share, my hope is to empower your dream, to give passion to your purpose, and to guide you back into the process of living out your truth with all of the creativity and passion you were gifted with by God.

These steps are not a to-do list or a checklist for you to follow. They're not something you need to climb, like traditional steps of stone. Instead, they're the foundational movements of a dance that is meant for you to learn and then build upon yourself—in your own unique way.

Life is a dance. It is glorious and beautiful. But it is not easy.

It takes work. It takes collaboration, understanding, and guidance. It begs for choreography, for vision, for direction. And every dancer—every dreamer—at some point finds that they need a little help: a hand up, some inspiration, a reminder that what they feel is okay to feel. Encouragement that it's okay, even glorious, to fall down now and then, because in the falling we learn to grow and step into what's next—which is always better than what was, as long as we let it be.

As you're about to see, when we dance in life, when we're living our truth, when we feel the rhythm, when we're in it and giving it our all, the forces that want us to not be ourselves become powerless. They get pushed away.

God's gifts start flowing to the surface.

And we *rise*.

From behind the curtain, through the hush of the world, as the light gets ready to shine on each one of us.

Together, we rise.

STEP 1

Dare To Dream

I wanted to dance.

That's all I knew.

My mother always said, "You came out wanting to dance!"

In fact, I'm pretty sure I was dancing before I even came into this world. My mother used to complain about her stretch marks: "I didn't have them with Debbie. I didn't have them with Karen. *You* did this." But now when we look at them, we laugh. She's like, "Laurieann, you left this on my belly because you were dancing."

"I was choreographing in the womb!" I say. "I was doing eight-counts of life in there."

Both my mom and my older sisters remember me, at a very young age, putting a towel on my head and creating performances while dancing around the house. I apparently learned just from watching TV. Diana Ross and Lola Falana (of "Whatever Lola Wants, Lola Gets" fame) captivated me, so I would mimic them and just dance and dance.

My mom had enrolled both of my older sisters in dance classes before I came along, and both of them rejected it. She vowed she wasn't going to waste her money on classes anymore. But when I was five years old and realized that such a thing as dance classes existed, I asked for lessons. I *begged* for lessons. And she felt she had no choice but to say yes.

I can still hear the sound of her beautiful Jamaican accent saying, "Okay, wouldn't it be that the other two didn't want it and this one wants it, and now I can barely afford it?" But she found a way to put me in class at a dance studio where I was able to pursue my dream: to become a professional dancer.

By the time I was eight, my mom was dropping me off at the Jack Lemmon Dance Studio in Toronto every Saturday morning at eight, and I'd take every class—jazz, tap, ballet, *everything*—'til she came to pick me up at four in the afternoon. I don't remember any of the other kids staying all day like that, taking all the classes, but I was *in*.

I think it actually made it easier for my mom because on Saturdays she wouldn't have to deal with me. Saturday was her one day to get all the grocery shopping and everything else done, and there was so much to do that she was always late picking me up.

The other kids would say, "Goodbye, Laurie," and the teachers would say, "Bye, Laurie!"

"Goodbye," I'd reply to my teachers, until the last one was locking the door while I waited outside.

"Laurie, you gonna be okay? Your mom's gonna come?"

"Yeah, she'll be here," I said.

I had absolute faith that my mom would show up, so I wasn't afraid to wait in a parking lot alone. When everyone was gone, I would *still* be dancing—literally tap-dancing in the parking lot—until I saw her pull up in her little Honda Civic. She always brought a sugar doughnut for me, so it was worth the wait. (Hence my obsession with sugar doughnuts to this day.) In my mind, the doughnut was a reward, but it was really just so I wouldn't get mad at her for being late.

It's interesting looking back on it. Somebody else might have been stressed out that their mom had such a hard time paying for lessons and couldn't afford to arrange her schedule so she wouldn't have to pick them up late. Instead I found joy in what it *was*, because I was so focused on my dream, and I loved to dance *so much*. That's all that mattered to me.

Sometimes I had to teach the younger kids in that dance school in order to chop some money off the price of my own classes. I wasn't ready to be a teacher. I was just a kid! I wanted to learn, not teach. Plus, I didn't see the value in becoming a teacher or choreographer. I didn't know the power of what those things could be. But I didn't complain about it like some kids might. I was just so glad that I got to dance every Saturday. That's all that mattered.

My passion was bigger than my circumstance.

Today when I work with artists, I remind them that it's their passion that will sustain them—through rehearsals, through rejections, through the climb, through the hard times.

My mom will tell you that I was a happy baby; I was never, ever going to be bitter or a diva. These things were not part of my makeup. But I don't see my positive attitude as something that's innate and automatic. I believe—in fact, I *know*—that my positivity, my perseverance, my drive, and my resiliency all came from within. It came from my passion, my dream. As long as I was in touch with that dream, that feeling of what I loved and what I wanted, I was *good*.

The Power of Your Passion

Staying in touch with our dreams matters more than most of us ever talk about.

My mom had a hard time paying for my dance lessons even

As long as I was in
touch with that *dream*,
that *feeling* of what
I loved and what I
wanted, I was *good*.

though my parents both worked full-time jobs. My dad, who's passed on now, worked as an electrician, and my mom worked for Xerox of Canada.

Working for Xerox was *not* her dream. They're a fine company and treated her well, but her passion was not for printers.

Her passion was for design.

My mom wanted to be a fashion designer, but *her* mom told her that wasn't a "real" job. It wasn't a "real" career. She was flat out told that she could not be a designer, so she chose another path. But designing was still her passion. It was still her dream. So she tried along the way to touch that feeling that she knew was ultimately herself.

My mom designed and sewed a lot of the clothes my sisters and I wore to school. There were times when she stretched even further and offered some of her designs for sale to friends and acquaintances. She'd organize little fashion shows in our living room, and I'd model for them. I got my own feel for fashion, for costuming, for patterns—the skills I would later apply to my work for Lady Gaga, for Puffy, for Katy Perry—from *her*.

My mom is retired now, living in Jamaica, but she's still designing beach cover-ups and dresses. We're working on opening a shop for her down there. Throughout my career I've worn her designs, and it brings tears to my eyes because it makes me so proud. It's such an incredible feeling whenever someone asks me, "Who are you wearing?" and I tell them, "My mom designed this!"

Even though she was deterred, she never let go of her dream. And she promised herself that when she had kids, she was never, *ever* going to stop them from pursuing their passions. That's why she worked so hard and stretched her budget so far to keep me enrolled in dance classes. But it's also why she let me be my full-on creative self in just about any way I wanted.

For example, when I was seven (my mom tells me, because I do not remember this), I kept a big cardboard box in the basement, and I kept choreographing myself in and out of this box. The basement was my dad's cave. It was where he played his records and hung out with his friends. So my dad was like, "What is this box doing in my basement? I'm going to throw this box out."

"No, Daddy. Daddy, no!" I cried, and my mother didn't let him.

Finally, one day, he asked me and my mom, "What is it that you want with this box?"

My mom took that opportunity to ask me what exactly it was I was doing, going in and out of this box all the time, and I told them, *"I'm birthing myself into the world!"*

Like I said, I don't remember this. But my mom remembers it vividly because it was a perfect reflection of my sense of play, my sense of creativity. It might have made no sense to anyone but me, but she saw it as something beautiful.

Those of you who've followed my career may recall that many years later I did something similar in my creative work with Lady Gaga. I'll talk later about the power of that moment, but I bring it up here because, *wow!* Something I didn't even remember—something my mom didn't tell me about until after it had shown up in my creative choices a few decades later—was clearly inside me, waiting to come out. That creative play that might have seemed like silly kid stuff to somebody else was part of my process. To me, that's proof that in the process is the perfection, the power, the greatness—and that needs to be celebrated.

Had my mom let my dad throw out the box and said, "You

need to go upstairs and study your books," I don't know if I would have ever had enough of that box in me to later create something that would move the world.

When I was little, my older sister Debbie had an assignment to choreograph a jazz routine for gym class. She didn't know what to do, so she asked me. Apparently, I jumped right in and came up with a routine for her. When I taught it to her, I yelled at her like choreographers tend to do: "Yeah . . . lunge, snap, lunge, snap. Ball-change, hitchy-koo, ball-change." (Again, I was so young that I can't recall any of this happening; she told me about it many years later.) Even though I was too young to be a teacher or a choreographer, and maybe didn't even know what a choreographer was, I somehow created the language to teach her a routine so well that she could remember it, teach it to others, and get an A. My sister embraced the fact that I loved to dance, and she trusted it, just as my mom did.

No one at home stopped me from exploring and expressing, no matter what it was. Simply being allowed to stay in touch with and express my dreams, my inner voice, my creative spirit, allowed me to become what only God knew I was capable of becoming.

It's an interesting lesson for parents, I think. Kids tend to be obsessed with certain things, and a lot of times when a child reaches a certain age, the parent is like, "Okay, you've done enough of that." "It's time for you to get serious." "It's time for you to stop playing in the box." And they stop the child from their "childish" thing because of their own perception of what it is. Maybe they haven't been trained to know that a child's obsession might be a gift, and that it's okay if it's *different*, and that it's separate from who they are as the parent. But my mother knew to give way to my passion. Because of what had happened to her dreams, there was *no way* she was gonna stop me.

She didn't even stop me from my obsession with Barbies. I had the Barbie Dreamboat, the Barbie Dreamhouse, and the Barbie Corvette. I turned my crawl space under the basement stairs into a whole Barbie *world*. The older I got, the more childish it must have seemed to my family, but no one stopped me from playing with those Barbies. And guess what? That obsession would turn up in my professional life later, too, with Nicki Minaj. (I'll share more about that in the pages ahead!)

As I got older, I utilized this type of creativity from my childhood over and over in my work. Creativity would turn out to be one of my gifts, which would expand as God expanded my circumstances. I found that I could use the ability I developed as a child to imagine what each artist's world would look like.

Being a creative person who inspires other artists is a big part of who I am. That doesn't mean that's who *you* are, or who *you* should be. Your world doesn't have to look like mine. In fact, it *can't* look like mine. Each artist, each person, has their own world—one that comes from the inside out. That's part of what I want to inspire you to see.

This may take time to understand, because society doesn't want us to understand what it is we're missing. Say you're a doctor. You have to ask yourself, if that's *not* what you—from the inside out—want to be, why are you one? Is it because you think it gives you status in the community? Is it because it's what your parents wanted you to be? Is it because doctors are revered and respected, or that they earn a certain amount of money? Or are you a doctor because, deep down inside, you're a caregiver and a healer, and being a doctor is all about expressing that special gift that God gave you?

Entertainers have the ability to evoke joy and faith and inspiration, and to touch people and heal people. In a way, that makes them a different kind of doctor. That pursuit is just as worthwhile a gift, and if being an entertainer is your gift, I hope you're pursuing it. If you aren't, why not? Is it because you don't think you can earn a living at it? Should that be the sole measure of whether you pursue what's powerful and passionate in you?

Sometimes it feels like everyone's trying to be someone else, someone other than who they are from the inside out, because people tell them that that's what they need to do or are supposed to do in order to be successful.

I want to argue that there's another way to live.

Even if you're far from where you thought you wanted to be when you were young, when you were most creative, when you were most passionate about something that's maybe faded into a distant memory—whatever that something is, I want to argue that it's important to dig in and touch it again, live it again, embrace it again. Because when we do, life gets better. Fuller. Richer. I want you to recognize that the passion inside you is a gift from God, which can express itself in all sorts of ways and can give you a level of success and completeness that's greater than anything society's rules and games and false measures of success can ever offer.

We'll get to all of that in the chapters ahead. I promise.

What's miraculous to me is that I *wasn't* deterred. Not early on, and not as I got older either. Maybe it's because my mom had my back and let me be who I wanted to be. Or maybe God gave me that gift so I would be able to share it with you now. But by

The *passion* inside
you is a gift from God,
which can *express*
itself in all sorts of
ways and can give you
a level of *success* and
completeness that's
greater than *anything*
society's rules and games
and false measures of
success can ever offer.

the time the naysayers started to show their faces in my life, my own creativity—and my dream and my passion—was far too big for any one person to shut it down.

Thank God for that. Because I'm telling you, when the Dreamkillers come, they come *strong*.

Don't Let Them Kill Your Dream

Mr. Christopher was one of the teachers at my dance school, and he was a good teacher when it came to technique and movement. But one day when I was eleven or twelve, he looked at me—the only black girl in his ballet class—and told me, "You will never be a ballerina."

I was confused and shocked. I was the best dancer in the class. That's not bragging; it was just a fact. We were kids, not professionals, but I treated dance almost like I was a professional, from very early on. I worked harder and studied more and practiced longer and took it more seriously than anyone else. I *loved* the dance. I wanted it. I lived it. I *breathed* it.

I was sure that Mr. Christopher knew that I was the best dancer in the class, too, so I couldn't understand why he would say something like that.

"What do you mean?" I asked him.

"Your feet are flat," he told me. "Your back is too arched."

He wasn't talking about my abilities. He was talking about my body, and how what I looked like didn't fit the idea of what a ballerina was supposed to look like—in *his* mind.

It's as if he were saying, "Black girl, what are you trying to be the white swan for?"

I couldn't change the fact that I was black. I couldn't help that I had a more athletic build than the typical white ballerina. My parents were from the West Indies. From Jamaica, the land of Usain Bolt. One day, I would appreciate the natural athleticism that came from that DNA, and how my build would allow me to leap higher and move bigger. But Mr. Christopher was saying that I didn't fit the mold of what *he* thought a ballerina was supposed to look like.

Everything in ballet is turning from the inside out. Because of the curve of my back and the shape of my body, my butt would literally be in the way of moving the way a traditional ballerina should be able to move or look; because of the flatness of my feet (which weren't even done developing yet), I would never achieve the kind of point that the Russian-influenced version of the ballet called for. (By the way, my feet eventually developed an arch, and I can point my toes beautifully today!)

That right there, that one moment in Mr. Christopher's class, could have killed it for me. It could have derailed me. It could have made me give up on my dream—if I had listened to him.

I didn't. I ignored him.

My dream was bigger than his vision, so my spirit was undeterred.

But I know a lot of people *do* listen. Their dreams get killed, just like that.

I think teachers sometimes don't realize the incredible power they hold to lift kids up with even a few encouraging words. Why use that power to derail dreams when dreams are what drive us, all of us, to keep moving forward? In the so-called real world, where people expected ballet dancers to look a certain way, I'm sure that Mr. Christopher's words seemed accurate to him. I was definitely not a tall, white, Russian-looking girl. But my dream is what drove me, and the dream is what leads to a truth that's much bigger than the limited view of what's already been done, and what everyone already expects a thing to look like.

When it comes to creativity and artistry and even industry, what's new is what we eventually see as great. Imitation, repetition, the same old same old can be beautiful and comfortable and sustainable for a time, sure. But the breakthrough artists, the visionaries, the ones who inspire us to new heights? They're not only doing what's been done; they're doing what's *never* been done. The great ones don't necessarily look like or act like or sing like or dance like anyone who came before them—because they're uniquely themselves! Shouldn't we be encouraging more of *that*?

I wasn't able to articulate any of this as a kid. I just knew that what Mr. Christopher told me felt wrong. This was *my* dream, and who was he to say I couldn't do it? What does any other person know about the power of what God gave me? The path God put me on? The plans that God might have for me or for anyone else?

God's plans for me were bigger than a man's.

Why I had such confidence in myself and in what I wanted to do is beyond me. But I do think it has something to do with the fact that my mom didn't limit my creativity, which meant that my mind was free to imagine more than what one older white male teacher saw in me.

It's okay for you to be passionately free with your creativity too. I give you permission! But I don't need to be the one to give you permission; God gave it to you when he gave you that creativity in the first place. He gave you those dreams, those desires, those ideas that come into your head that tell you how you can do things differently or make things better or design something you love or dance like nobody's ever danced before. Those are *your* dreams, and *your* ideas, and *your* passions, and you have every right to express them and pursue them and live and breathe them however you choose. They're your connection to God himself! When you embrace your creativity, when you dare to dream, when you think about what you want to be, who you could be, who you are at your core, you're touching truth. And that truth will carry you. It will lift you. It will guide you.

When it came to my mom, touching her dream even in the smallest of ways lifted her through the tough times she faced, and it still lifts my mom to this day. Just as focusing on *my* dream, *my* passion, *my* truth, lifted me right past Mr. Christopher's limited view of the world and into something bigger than he ever could have imagined.

Brown-Skinned Girls, Like Me

When I was twelve going on thirteen, my mother took me to see the Alvin Ailey American Dance Theater perform at the O'Keefe Centre in Toronto. I sat there in awe, watching the most beautiful brown-skinned girls dancing in pointe shoes with the power of all the older white girls in my ballet school—but there was no judgment.

At my ballet school teachers like Mr. Christopher tried to tell me I couldn't do that, but now I saw other girls doing it, and they looked like me! They performed *Revelations* and *Stack-Up*, which included movements and choreography far beyond any modern ballet I'd ever seen. I was like, "Mom, what is *that*?"

From that moment, I knew where I wanted to go: the Alvin Ailey American Dance Theater in New York City. I had only ever been to New York City once, for a day or so on a field trip. I saw the billboard for *A Chorus Line* in Times Square, and it inspired me so much. (Not the show—just the billboard!) The city was so exciting, but I had no idea what it would mean to live there. I had never even been to the United States other than that one time.

I knew I had to graduate high school first, and I knew I'd have to be good in order to get into the Ailey program. I had no idea what it would take to audition, or how we would ever pay for a school like that, or anything else. None of that mattered. The dream was implanted in my heart. I just kept thinking, *If all those other girls with skin like mine and bodies like mine can fly onstage like that, why can't I?*

My dream of becoming a dancer was now augmented with the specific goal of going to Alvin Ailey, and that goal was enough to carry me straight through high school. With the dream in mind, I worked hard—like I always had—and auditioned and attended Claude Watson School for the Arts in Toronto, where my dream and my talents would be treated with as much honor and attention as the academic subjects in which other kids thrived in other types of high schools.

I wanted to learn technique. I wanted to be the best dancer I could be.

My mother always told me, "You can do whatever you want, but seek out the training that will make you the best."

Dancing *Swan Lake* wasn't my dream; dancing traditional ballet was what led to the *evolution* of my dream. Wanting to be a dancer led me to wanting to do it *all*. I wanted to master the technique of ballet, but I *loved* jazz, tap, modern, and (eventually) hip-hop.

When I go to the ballet today, and I love it so much, I can't help but think about what a visionary like George Balanchine accomplished in cofounding the New York City Ballet and the School of American Ballet. He moved the art form forward from the purely classical vision he grew up with in Saint Petersburg, Russia, and turned it into something neoclassical starting in the 1930s. Yet I also wonder how much his vision might have grown and changed had he lived beyond 1983. He was working with what he had to work with at the time, based on what he grew up with, and he evolved ballet through his connections to Broadway and the composers of his era. Balanchine made the ballet more modern, but why didn't he continue to make it even *more* modern and diverse and reflective of the city and world around him after he found such great success? What would have happened if a girl like me had walked into his studio? Maybe he just never met a Laurieann Gibson or some other young black girl who was dedicated to the craft with her whole heart and soul. Maybe meeting someone like one of us would have inspired him and taken his vision to a whole new place. Who knows?

In all these years, ballet in America (and in Canada too) has stuck incredibly close to the vision Balanchine created nearly a century ago. So many producers and theater directors don't want to mess with the kind of success he achieved. They see it as something untouchable, lightning in a bottle that can never be re-created. But artists, *true* artists, are almost always constantly evolving, constantly becoming *more*, better, different, bigger as they react to the inspiration from and influences of the world around them. That's just part of being an artist.

In my experience, it's rarely the artists themselves who stop art from growing and evolving; it's the people who now make money off them. So many times in my career I've seen art stopped in its tracks—not by the artists, but by those in charge, usually men with money who want to invest in what is already proven. But they lack the vision and judgment to see that art is meant to continuously push to new levels.

I want you to hear what I tell my artists: Don't look in the world for evidence of what you're dreaming to be. What you're dreaming might be entirely new, and you don't want to stop that!

I can't help but wonder how many artists have been shut down because of the ripple effects of that kind of institutional oppression—the oppression of Dreamkillers who do everything in their power to keep things just as they already are. Because of the trickle-down effect of the power we give those in charge of our arts institutions, how many other little girls encountered a Mr. Christopher and were told they couldn't be ballerinas because of what they looked like, no matter how talented they were?

How many little black girls gave up on even *dreaming* of becoming the lead ballerina in a ballet company before Misty Copeland came along and broke that barrier? It's so sad to even think about.

How many girls like me didn't have a mom who took them to see Alvin Ailey to show them a different view, a different interpretation, a different manifestation of the possibility of their dreams?

I didn't see something less than Balanchine in Alvin Ailey. I didn't align with any of the snobbery of believing one genre of dance was better than another. Instead, I saw something bigger in Ailey for *me*: a different passion, a way of breaking the mold.

Just as Balanchine took ballet to a different place, Ailey shattered what Mr. Christopher told me about what dance could be.

I'm here to tell you that the Dreamkillers, the ones who say you can't, are wrong. There is *always* another way, a different interpretation, a different dream that they don't understand. And that different perspective might not be something you can go see somewhere, because it hasn't even been created yet. That vision has to come from *you*. And often, those are the greatest visions of all.

On My Own

Ideology and traditions and limited views weren't the only things working against my dream as I grew into a young adult in the Toronto suburbs. As I neared the end of high school, my parents went through a divorce.

My mom was so overwhelmed by what was happening in her own life that she didn't have the time or energy to help walk me through the process of applying to Alvin Ailey. What little money my mom had to support my dream now seemed to all but vanish too. She had all she could do just to keep herself going, let alone have time to help me with things like filling out an application to a dance school that seemed so far away from anything we'd known in my family.

So I applied by myself. I sent an audition tape. I gave it everything I had. I got the recommendations from teachers I trusted and loved.

My sisters helped me with some of it, but I knew I had no choice but to figure things out on my own if I wanted to make my dream a reality.

I just did it.

And I got in.

At the end of the summer of 1989, my big sister Debbie dropped me off at the bus station, and at seventeen years old, all on my own, I took a Greyhound bus to New York City.

That moment was the beginning of everything. *Everything.* So much more than I ever imagined possible. And it all started because I dared to dream—and I held on to that dream as I grew.

STEP 2

Empower Your Purpose

When I boarded that Greyhound bus bound for New York, I didn't have a place to live. I didn't have a proper student visa in place either, which meant I would be in America illegally if I spent more than three months in school without applying for a type of visa I couldn't afford. I didn't know anyone in the big city, and I barely had a penny to my name. I just believed this was what I was meant to do.

Down deep in my heart, I had this undeniable feeling that if I followed my dream, this *one big dream*, then the circumstances would fall into place.

Of course, I didn't just wish and hope it would happen without making any effort. That's not how dreams work. I did everything I could to empower my ability to live out what I felt was my purpose. That meant not only putting in the work as a dancer, practicing 'til the soles of my feet were raw and my toes were bloody and every bone in my body ached, but also working to make the money I needed to pay for school when it became clear that my divorcing parents wouldn't be able to contribute to my tuition.

The bill? Thirteen thousand dollars.

That's a lot of money for a seventeen-year-old kid. For that, I needed to hustle.

Given the circumstances, it might have been easier to let it go, to put it off, to get mad at my parents for not being there when I needed their help, to use the divorce or their lack of money as an excuse not to do what I wanted to do, what I was *called* to do, what excited me more than anything else I could even imagine at that point. But how could I turn away from that feeling? How could I turn away from that voice inside me that told me again and again that Alvin Ailey was where I belonged?

I couldn't. So I got to work.

I auditioned for a good-paying gig that summer at our theme park, Canada's Wonderland. I had one bodysuit that I used for every audition because it was the only one I owned. It got so dirty I had to dye it so I could keep wearing it. It came out sort of tie-dyed teal blue, and I just prayed that nobody would realize that some of the shading was because of the stains.

I guess no one noticed, because I got a job as a dancer in the Canterbury Theatre, where I performed in little off-Broadway-type shows multiple times per day. The hours were long, and the shows could be exhausting, but I wasn't about to complain. I was dancing and making good money. Even if it wasn't exactly what I wanted to be doing, it was still *dance*. It was still in the field I wanted to pursue. To me, being on the path toward the thing is a big part of eventually *doing* the thing.

Plus, working wasn't something new to me. I'd been working part-time since I was fifteen. At first I took a job at McDonald's, and then I worked at the Laura Secord ice cream factory, cracking open packets of flavors that go in the ice cream and sending them down the line. While I was working both of those jobs, I was like, *Mm-mm, no way, I cannot do this.* I mean, I *did* it—I woke up early, got on the bus, and went to the restaurant or factory—but I knew those jobs were taking me someplace else. They served as a confirmation that I *had* to make it, because I did not want to do that type of work for the rest of my life.

Honestly, it was one of those early things that let me know

what a "flag" is. To me, a flag is something that pops up and lets you know what you don't want to do. It's not necessarily a red flag, as in something that's bad for you, but it's something that doesn't align with your spirit. A flag is an alignment problem, a signal that it's time for a directional shift. The moment when you think to yourself, *Ohhh, I gotta make a turn! What I'm doing is not part of my dream plan.*

The flag didn't pop up because working at McDonald's or an ice cream factory is a bad thing. I had the best time when I was there. I always smiled when I said, "Would you like fries with that?" but I just knew, *This is not for me.*

My capacity told me, *I have more for you than this.*

There is no judgment at all in that statement, by the way. Everyone's capacity is different. Everyone's purpose is different. I say to my students and clients and mentees all the time, "Your capacity matches your destiny. It matches the dream that you've been given. It's all in tandem. You're not gonna have an appetite for something that is not destined to produce what it is you want to become."

If you don't have an appetite for it, whatever *it* is, then you're not gonna produce what you need in order to become it. Too many people fight that.

So I'm not putting anyone down, no matter what job they have. I just knew that those jobs were stepping-stones to where my purpose was empowering me to go. We all learn lessons as we make our way through life, and whatever you're doing right now is definitely teaching you something you need. We're all in the right place all the time, even if we're not following our dreams. What you're doing at this moment is helping to empower your purpose—if you let it.

If you're managing a McDonald's, that might be the key education that leads you to managing your own brand someday. It might be perfectly in alignment with the appetite you have to produce what your destiny is. Or maybe you're the best McDonald's employee there is, and *that's* your destiny. And that's wonderful if that's your dream! It's amazing to be able to say, "I am grateful for the 401(k) plan and the chance to serve as the biggest ambassador of this brand in my neighborhood." A manager of a McDonald's could be sustaining the entire corporation in a way that we don't even know. The capacity to serve that brand and provide jobs in that community is astounding, and when that manager raises five kids that are about to go out there and follow their dreams to be something "more," then clearly that dream was sufficient. It was fantastic! We need to respect and honor that. It's not less than what a Steve Jobs or a Quincy Jones has done. Whatever your dream is, be brave enough and bold enough to believe in the value of that—and *own it*. Don't let anyone challenge what produces your joy, your happiness, and your confidence.

And if what you're doing now is *not* your passion, I want to encourage you to dig deeper and to question, "Where does this position I'm in now fit in with my dream?"

I knew that my summer job as a dancer was just another stepping-stone to getting to New York City. God gave me the clarity of vision on that. I was in the process of the dream, which made me more effective in the job I was in. I automatically got more enjoyment from that work because I knew it was part of the larger process.

What you don't know is what God is perfecting in you while you're in this part of the process. So embrace it, and do what you have to do in order to keep moving toward the dream.

Whatever your dream is,
be *brave* enough and
bold enough to believe
in the value of that—
and *own* *it*. Don't let
anyone challenge what
produces your *joy*,
your *happiness*, and
your *confidence*.

Fallback? What Fallback?

After the first few weeks at Canada's Wonderland, I looked at my take-home pay, did some math, and realized I wasn't going to make it. No matter how many hours I put in at the Canterbury Theatre and how much I was able to save, I didn't see how I could possibly save $13,000 by the end of the summer.

So I prayed to God to help me find a way.

And he *did*.

I read a notice that Patti LaBelle was filming a movie in Toronto called *Sing*. The casting agents needed actors—specifically, actors who could dance—who looked like me for a classroom scene in the movie. So I did what dancers do: I auditioned, and I got it.

That one acting gig paid $6,000—nearly half the tuition I needed. From one job!

It felt like magic. Like it was meant to be. Like an affirmation that I was on the right path.

Guess what? It *was*. I was learning by experience that when you follow the road toward your God-given gifts, God provides.

My mom didn't take my sisters and me to church every Sunday, but she was raised Catholic in Jamaica, and God was always acknowledged in our home. I even went to Catholic school when I was a little girl, but I didn't like it, and I switched over to public school as soon as I could. I wasn't saved—I didn't have a personal relationship with Jesus yet—but I always believed I was *called*.

Before I left for New York, my mom got into metaphysics and the power of positive thinking, so my household was very "Love and speak life" and "When you fall down, you get back up." My mom gave me a lot of metaphysical books when I went to New

York, and because of what I read in those books and what my mom would say, I would speak positive statements over myself, phrases like "Thank you, God, for my limitless financial flow" or "Thank you, God, that all things are in divine order." I would say these phrases over and over, and I even wrote them down.

Eventually I realized that this—thanking God, speaking positively, reiterating affirmations—was part of my relationship with the Spirit of Christ. In the years ahead, I would come to understand that it is the Word of God that is transformative and has the power beyond the power, but even back then I realized I was training myself to speak life over myself instead of giving in to negative thoughts.

That positivity, combined with the creativity from my childhood, definitely played a part in what some people might say was my "bravery"—or maybe my "naivete"—in going to New York on nothing but a wing and a prayer at the age of seventeen.

Our extended family was like, "You're going to let her get on a Greyhound bus?" And my mother said, "I have to." Maybe if my parents weren't so consumed by their divorce, they would have looked at the circumstances and said, "No way!" But they didn't. My mother saw my passion, and because of her own experience, she refused to stand in my way. There was so much power in the fact that she spoke that support, versus her own doubts and fears, into her child's life.

So many parents stop their creative kids from growing by giving them warnings: "Well, it's great that you like music, but make sure you get a degree and a job you can fall back on."

The *fallback*. The creation of an option. An option that was never intended to be a part of your conversation.

I didn't have a fallback. I didn't apply to any other schools.

I didn't have a job waiting for me if I failed. I didn't give myself the option of failing.

I can't tell you how many people asked me, "Do you have a fallback?" I always responded, "I don't *need* a fallback. This is what I do. This is what I love!"

I know this sounds scary, and it goes against what society seems to tell us, but believe me: having a fallback is not safer—not for your soul, anyway. Having a fallback creates an option. And more often than not, that option becomes the choice because the fallback is the easier thing to do. The fallback allows us to convince ourselves that we're *not* going to be what we know we're meant to be.

Why do we feel that we need something to fall back on? Maybe it's because others tell us not to accept the dream given to us by God; not to accept the passion of that dream, the *feeling* in that dream.

There's no shame in choosing the fallback. It happens to almost everyone! Maybe the fallback is part of your process. But there's also no reason to accept that it's permanent. Even if you've taken the fallback road, you can go back to your dream anytime you want to and *empower it*. The choice is up to you.

When you open your eyes to the possibility of empowering your dream, you just might find that the dream created an opportunity for you that you didn't imagine. The fact is, whatever path you are on right now might just be a fulfillment of something you didn't see—but *God* saw. As you stick to the dream that's specific to you, the one that has your name on it, you can celebrate the twists and turns in your process because they're all leading to what your dream really is.

For example, it would turn out that I was in ballet class *not*

Whatever *path* you are
on right now might just
be a *fulfillment* of
something you didn't
see—but *God* saw.

to be a ballerina but to become a choreographer, a director, and a visionary who unleashes the fulfillment of dreams in other artists like *you*. But I didn't know that at the time. How could I?

I followed the feeling of the dream, almost blindly, to New York City. Sometimes I look back on that girl and think, *Who were you? How did you do that?* Why *did you do that?* Then I remember that I held on to the dream so tightly that I chose the dream over the circumstances. I faced the situation as fearlessly and creatively as the little girl who birthed herself out of a cardboard box.

I unflinchingly believed the dream would come true—and it did.

Big City Lights

I arrived in New York City with $13,094 in my bank account—and $13,000 of that was going straight to my tuition.

I had one great big green-and-yellow duffel bag full of all the clothes and belongings I could carry. Actually, it weighed so much I *couldn't* carry it. I took a yellow cab from the bus station at 42nd Street to Alvin Ailey, which at that time was located beneath the Minskoff Theatre at 44th and Broadway—where, coincidentally, *A Chorus Line* was playing. When I got out of the cab, I had to kick-slide that duffel bag down the sidewalk—in the middle of Times Square. *Kick, kick, kick.* No one offered to help. No one even looked at me funny. It was somehow normal to see a girl kicking a giant duffel in the heart of the Broadway shuffle.

The security officer at the door of the school saw me coming and said, "Are you trying to get in here?"

"Yes," I said. *Kick, kick.*

"Here you go now," he said, and he lifted my bag, opened the door for me, and got me settled in the lobby.

Even though all I'd done so far was kick and drag my duffel into the lobby, I was *there*!

I knew only one person at Alvin Ailey, a dancer from Toronto named Abe, whom I met at Canada's Wonderland. In one phone call we had, Abe had told me there were always people at the school looking for roommates. I didn't know how to find any of those people, so I just took it on faith and figured he'd help me figure it out when I got to Ailey. But when I got there, Abe was in class. I'd have to wait all day for him to come out and help me. So I walked into the foreign-student advisor's office, unannounced, and let her know I had arrived.

The first thing she asked me was "Where are you staying?"

I hadn't listed a New York address on my paperwork.

"Oh, Abe has someone I can stay with," I said. "I'll talk to him when he's out of class."

The advisor reminded me that I'd need to apply for a student visa and have it in place before the end of my third month. I didn't have the heart to tell him that a student visa wasn't gonna work for me. You can't hold down a job on a student visa, and I needed to work in order to pay my rent and expenses. And I didn't know how I would apply for any other kind of visa that would allow me to work, because those visas required lawyers and, therefore, money.

When Abe finally came out of class and I asked him if he knew anyone I could stay with, he was shocked: "Laurieann, I thought you were going to find a roommate before you came down from Toronto!"

He looked worried for me. He didn't know anyone who was looking for a roommate, he said. "But maybe someone posted something on the student message board."

We walked over to this board on the wall that had all kinds of notices and notes pinned to it. They were mostly for gigs and auditions and things, but there was one note that said "Roommate Wanted." Just as we were standing there looking at it, a girl walked up and said, "That's mine. Are you looking?"

I told her I'd just come down from Toronto, and she said, "Great! You can come stay with me." Her name was Felicia, and her apartment was in Queens. The number of trains we had to take to get there was mind-blowing. I had no idea how I would ever remember all the stations and transfers. But she helped me with my duffel bag as we climbed the stairs to her sixth-story walk-up railroad apartment that night, and I was grateful.

If you live outside New York City, you might not know what a railroad apartment is. The rooms are all set up like a series of railroad cars, in one straight line from the front door to the back wall, one after another. You have to walk through each room to get to the next. I slept in the dining room, right next to the kitchen, and Felicia had the main bedroom, the one with all the privacy at the back of the apartment. The only bathroom was between her room and mine. We had another roommate, too, a girl from Japan. So if either of them went to the kitchen, they had to go through my room to get there, and the girl from Japan had to walk through my room anytime she had to go to the bathroom. There truly was no privacy at all! But I was so happy just to be on the floor with a sleeping bag and my duffel bag—no bed, no dresser, no nothing—because I was in *New York City*. And the next day I woke up and went to my very first dance class at Alvin Ailey.

That first class felt bigger than life. Like I was a small ladybug in the biggest blades of grass that were taller than the Empire State Building. Yet even among the giants, I was *seen*. It was everything. It was colorful. It was soulful. It was hot. I still remember how the studio smelled, the resin on the gray spring floor. And the sounds. We had live percussionists, and the drums beat through me, and the people moved so fast.

This was the *dance*, the dance of my *dreams*. And as soon as it was over, all I wanted to do was come back for more.

Felicia and I left at the same time that first day, so I didn't have a problem getting to school. But the second day I got so lost on the trains that I missed all my classes. I was traumatized. I had to beg for my teachers' forgiveness, and they all said, "Don't let it happen again."

The thought of getting kicked out of my dream school was enough to make me learn the ins and outs of the entire New York City subway system that very day. It's amazing how quickly you can learn something when your dreams are at stake.

I truly felt like I was in heaven those first two weeks—but I knew the clock was ticking. I needed to pay Felicia some rent if I was going to stay in that apartment. The eighty-four dollars I had to my name went quickly on subway fare and a little bit of food. I needed a job, but I knew I couldn't get one without a special visa that would allow me to work and go to school.

I felt stuck. So I prayed.

Miraculously, I met a Russian girl who waitressed at a well-known diner on 9th Avenue near Penn Station. She told me I could go interview there, since she, too, was working illegally. So two weeks after arriving in New York, I found myself waitressing at a greasy spoon.

I didn't know how to waitress. I didn't know how to lift a plate. I lied and told them I did. I knew I'd figure it out. And as quickly as I could, I did.

The diner was a crazy place. The short-order cooks were ex-cons. It was a whole movie in there. But I started making money, and the first thing I did after paying Felicia rent was to buy myself a futon and a pair of black cowboy boots.

Man, I looked at those cowboy boots for *weeks* until I could finally afford them. I was changing. I was *becoming.* I was feeling more confident in the dream, and I wanted those boots to help me stand out as my most authentic self. I wanted those boots to help let the world know that I was an individual. Cowboys are powerful. And these boots were black—they went with everything. Expressing myself by wearing different shoes from the other girls felt right. I was a creative, unique voice; an awkward bird, an individual, a dreamer, learning to own and wear and embrace my confidence. I was shedding the Toronto, and those boots matched my confidence that I was in New York City, at Alvin Ailey. My walk was changing, and wearing those boots became a reflection of what I was beginning to feel: bold, confident, happy, energetic.

As I settled in, I took some milk crates from the diner, cleaned them out, and built a dresser for myself. I put four on the bottom, then three, then two, then one, and that pyramid of milk crates held my jewelry, my perfume, my books, my T-shirts, my dance clothes, everything. It was literally my dresser. (Which is why today, when I walk into fancy stores and they have clean crates that look like milk crates, I'm like, "Excuse me if I don't wanna *buy* that. I used to clean out *real* milk crates that I got for free!")

I did whatever I had to do in order to empower my purpose: cleaning old crates, sleeping with no privacy, taking all of those trains every day—whatever it took. Because all day long, every day, I was *dancing*. I was moving. I was living and breathing my passion, surrounded by other talented dancers and unbelievably talented teachers who inspired me to reach places my body and soul had never *been* to.

My ballet class with Ms. Barbara Cole started at 9:00 a.m., followed by classes in various modern techniques: Horton, Graham, Dunham, and so on. I think I finished at 4:45 or 5:00 p.m. At first, the only shift I could get at the diner was from 11:00 p.m. to 6:00 a.m. on Mondays, Wednesdays, and Fridays. On days when I had to go to work, there wouldn't be enough time to go all the way to Queens and back on the trains, so I would nap at Ailey after classes were over, grab a bagel and a boxed juice, and then head straight to work. After finishing my shift the next morning, I'd get back to Ailey by 7:00 or 7:15, and while the janitors were opening up and cleaning, I'd sleep in the lounge. At 8:30 or 8:45, I'd put on my ballet clothes and go to Ms. Cole's class to start it all again. On those back-to-back days, I'd sleep again during lunch and wake up ready for the second half of the day.

Sometimes at the end of the day, when I was really tired, I would go to the diner early and sleep in the basement. It was quiet down there, but that privacy led to some unintended consequences: one day, the owner made a move on me. He tried to kiss me, and put his arms around me, and he looked at me like he wanted to do a whole lot more than that!

Yeah, it seemed like once I settled in, a young girl all on her own, some of *those* things came into play. It was nothing violent. I was able to easily say no. And in a strange way, in this case, I think it was all part of God's plan: not only did it teach me not to find myself alone in a room where a man might try something

I didn't want, but that moment that started as a flag turned into a boom-*kack* that sent me in a different direction and started a whole new conversation.

The owner of the diner, a Greek guy, wasn't a bad guy. He just liked me. There was something about my spirit and my spunk that led him to call me his *koukla*, which is Greek for "doll."

The more we talked, the more our friendship grew, with admiration and respect. I had turned eighteen by this time, and he was older than me, and I knew how that might look—but I fell in love with how he loved me and wanted to protect me. Maybe there was something that drew me to him because of my parents' divorce and my dad's leaving the picture, but for whatever reason, I fell in love with him, and he fell in love with me. There was a lot of secrecy involved, because in those days it just wasn't okay for a Greek man to be dating a black girl. Everyone at the diner knew about us, but he tried to keep it a secret from his family, he said, because they were just so traditional. (That's what he told me at the time.)

Looking back on it, I realize there was definitely something that didn't seem quite right about what we had together. I had a feeling—a feeling I ignored because I loved the protection of having him on my side. I won't lie: having a relationship with him got me better shifts. I wound up working 5:00 to 9:00 most nights, which was when all the big tips came in from the regular dinner crowd. And when my short-term visa ran out after three months and I was in serious danger of being sent back to Canada, he was the person who saved me.

I'll never forget when the foreign officer, a woman named Sarah, called me in to discuss my student visa. Right before the appointment, I went into the bathroom at school, got on my knees, and cried out to God, "I don't know what to do! Please help me!" I couldn't bear the thought of going home. Alvin Ailey was my *dream*. I was finally living my life, the one I was meant to live.

I finally pulled myself together and went downstairs, down a winding staircase to the offices, where Judith Jamison, the school's artistic director, stopped me and said, "Go back to class. Sarah has just been fired. We'll deal with your situation later."

Hallelujah! I felt bad for Sarah and had no idea what happened, but it was exactly the news I needed to hear that day. After that, my case must have gotten lost in the paperwork, because no one bothered me about my visa for the next six or eight months.

And you tell me there is no God?

By the time the school got around to asking me again, my boyfriend (the owner of the diner) had agreed to sponsor me. He paid attorneys to get me my very first O-1 visa—a visa for people with "extraordinary ability" in the arts, which allows them to both study and work in the United States.

It was good for three years.

Despite its unusual beginnings—and the heartache it would eventually cause me—being in that relationship allowed me to flourish in my purpose. It filled me with love and protection. It took away my worry and stress, and it allowed me to know for certain that I would be allowed to stay in New York and concentrate on my dancing.

So when I tell you that God is real, it's because I've experienced not having a plan and just trusting the gift that he gave me. At times I felt like I was echoing the story of the Wise Men: *This gift keeps drawing me this way. I know it's the right way to go, because God gave the gift to me.*

As broke as I was and as hard as I was working, I felt like I was living the freedom, the liberation, the alignment, the joy—everything that Jesus says we will have when he tells us, "I have come that they may have life, and that they may have it more abundantly" (John 10:10).

As I look back on my first couple of years in New York, I can't help but think about David, who is described in the Bible as "leaping and dancing before the LORD" (2 Samuel 6:16 KJV). Some have imagined that he danced before the Lord until his loincloth fell off! I swear, I was starting to experience that level of dance—that level of worship, that level of being, that level of joy, that level of breakthrough—at Alvin Ailey. It came in small moments, mostly in practice, whenever I hit new heights and stretched my gift to new levels. Musicians, dancers, artists of all kinds know that feeling, that high when it all just clicks and everything's in alignment, and the description of David just spotlights that feeling.

It's so striking to me that David *danced*. But why does the Bible depict his dance as the highest praise that could be given to God?

David was an original, somebody after God's own heart. That's *all of us*. That's me. That's you. So I believe God is telling *us* to dance too. I know I've felt it! *Dance like David, Laurieann.*

Your "dance" doesn't have to be what it is for anybody else.

And your "dance" doesn't have to be defined by the choices you've made so far.

When you empower your purpose, when you believe in your dream, you grow, you change, you see the world and all of your pursuits from new perspectives.

Like the first time I got the chance to dance at the O'Keefe Centre in Toronto as an Alvin Ailey dancer. I looked into that

Your "*dance*" doesn't
have to be what it is
for anybody else.
And your "*dance*"
doesn't have to be
defined by the choices
you've made so far.

audience from the stage instead of the other way around—and much to my surprise, I felt like, somehow, I was trapped inside a whole new box.

Breaking Free

For so many years, Alvin Ailey had been my North Star. The feeling I had when I thought about going to that school felt *right*. It felt like, "I am who I *am* when I'm in this feeling!"

By the time I was three-fifths of the way through my five-year program, I was aiming to join the second company, with my eyes set on making the first company, when I was given an opportunity to dance *behind* the first company in a series of shows. As younger, less experienced dancers, we were cast the way background actors would be cast in a major motion picture, or the chorus would be cast in a Broadway musical: we were given a role to play behind the stars. In this particular piece, the role was to be part of the "slave line."

The tour included one show up at the O'Keefe Centre—the very same venue where I had first laid eyes on the Alvin Ailey dancers when I was twelve years old. Standing in that auditorium, which at that time was still the pinnacle of the performing arts spaces in all of Toronto, was amazing. I had come full circle.

I was undulating, and I was contracting, and I was supposed to be serious as I played the part of one of these slaves. But this terrible feeling came over me. All of a sudden I was that little girl in the basement, birthing herself into the world, but I wasn't allowed to bust out of the box. My heart cried out, in the middle of the performance, *This is not me! I am not a slave!*

I couldn't understand why every night we were doing this piece that wasn't alive, that wasn't *today*. Why were we expressing a story out of the past when we were a modern dance troupe? I didn't understand that type of creativity; I didn't align with it. In time I would realize what felt so wrong: I didn't vibe with that particular brand of creativity because it wasn't my creation. I was supposed to be a choreographer *myself*.

At the time, the only thing I knew was the performance just felt wrong to me. It felt *uncomfortable*. Like, *Mm-mm, this is not right. I'm here! I'm an Alvin Ailey dancer! Why do I not feel happy? Why do I wanna break free of this slave line and shake my little tail feather and smile? My character is supposed to be upset and heavy, but that's not me. It's not me.*

I would come to understand that my unease was just a matter of God showing me that *my* gift was not *that*. Not that *that* wasn't great—it was! I look back now and I see the exquisite artistry of that work. It was an expression of that particular choreographer's vision, and that vision told a story of slavery and took it to new audiences who may not have cared about that history until they felt it through the dance. How amazing is the expression and storytelling ability of art in the hands of great artists? Art can give people a connected feeling to history like nothing else can. (Just look at what happened with the explosive popularity of *Hamilton* on Broadway all these years later.) But God needed me to understand that I had a capacity for something more, something different. Something that would pull me out of the slave line and let me shine in the way I'd always wanted to shine—even if I didn't yet fully understand in what way that might be.

My feelings confused me. I'd been praying to get into the second company. It was my obsession. And, by the way, I looked like the "perfect" black girl now. *You told me I wasn't good enough for ballet because I wasn't white enough*, I thought. Now? I was not only a good enough dancer but also the perfect image of an Alvin Ailey dancer, with the poise and the stance and the power that fit the profile of what Alvin Ailey dancers were supposed to be.

I still loved dancing at Ailey, and I prayed to be a part of it at the highest level. Yet a part of me didn't want to wear a leotard anymore. I didn't want to keep my hair in a tight bun. I wanted to burn my hair and let it stretch out in all directions. A part of me wanted to be the embodiment of the wild black girl, not the controlled, picture-perfect type of girl that fit the Alvin Ailey profile.

As human beings, how do we reconcile those kinds of conflicting feelings? We all have them at some point, no matter what education we're pursuing or what line of work we go into. Maybe you've felt it when you're really good at your job and you go for that promotion, but at the same time, there's a part of you that wants to quit and do something else. Or maybe you've experienced it when you're rockin' it in school, getting straight As and sitting at the top of your class, and all you can think is, *I wish I could drop out.*

Guess what? That pull you feel, that desire to do something more—I truly believe that is God calling, reminding you of the gifts he gave you and the *you* that is possible if you follow a path toward your greatest dreams and desires.

No sooner was I back in New York City than a path showed up right in front of me.

A friend told me about this audition she was thinking about going to for a hip-hop video featuring Heavy D & the Boyz. The casting director posted the audition notice on the Alvin Ailey wall, thinking it might be a good spot to find great dancers, but I'm pretty sure I'm the only girl from Alvin Ailey who wound up going.

I can't even fully explain why I went. I was studying ballet and modern and contemporary dance, and this was *hip-hop*. I was honestly like, "What is *that*?"

I was so engrossed in school and my work at the diner that I wasn't listening to the radio. I wasn't watching MTV. I wasn't paying attention to pop culture. The only music I listened to outside the music I was dancing to was whatever happened to be on the speakers at the diner, which meant I was completely out of touch with the massive shift in pop culture that was underway and the hip-hop takeover of pop music that was getting ready to explode.

I showed up wearing my fourth-period second company rehearsal outfit—tights and a black bodysuit, with my hair in a bun—which I quickly realized wasn't a "street" look. So I went into the bathroom, cut my tights off way up high on my thigh, took off the bottoms of them, and slipped on my black cowboy boots—the same ones I bought when I first bought my futon.

I walked into the room and said hi to all the guys. Heavy D & the Boyz were there, along with Puff Daddy. Not the Puff Daddy that everyone knows now; he wasn't famous yet. Still, he carried himself like he was in charge. He had a silver briefcase, and he handed me a business card, and he was like, "Hi. I'm the A&R of Uptown Records."

I was thinking, *A&R? What's that?* (I would learn later on that A&R stands for "artists and repertoire." It's the division of a record label that's responsible for talent scouting, as well as the artistic and commercial development of the recording artist.)

Choreographer Darrin Henson was there, too, just starting out. Later he would be on the forefront of creating all kinds of moves that would define pop culture, such as the choreography for NSYNC's "Bye, Bye, Bye" in the early 2000s.

I could tell that all these guys were laughing at me at first, but in a cute way—like they just didn't know what to make of this girl in the bun and the bodysuit and the cut-off tights and cowboy boots. I think they were used to girls being from the streets, creating their own looks, but they didn't know what I was.

When they pressed Play, I just moved to the music, using the sharpness and skills and expression I'd learned at Alvin Ailey, and they were like, "Yeah!" "Yes!" "We *want* her!" "She's killing it!" I picked up the Running Man on sight. The whole style of hip-hop came effortlessly to me.

Let this be a lesson for you.

I had never done hip-hop dance before. *Ever.* I didn't even know it existed before I heard about that audition. I wasn't from the streets. I didn't know Harlem or Brooklyn. I didn't know Heavy D. I didn't know *any* of that. I was the black girl who didn't belong anywhere. I didn't dress right. I didn't look the part. I wasn't trying to be sexy or selling my body to get the part, because I had a dancer's body at that age—thin and straight and strong and basically curve-less. But they wanted me because of exactly what I had to offer, which was technique and talent and confidence and drive and passion.

No matter what people say they want, from a résumé or anything else, what they *really* want—when they see it expressed, and when you're in the right place at the right time—is *you*. Your unique self! Your unique set of skills and talents and passions.

When you're in the right place and on the right path, everything aligns. Never forget that.

The Heavy D audition marked the beginning of me understanding the hip-hop culture—and marked the starting line for where I was headed next in my life.

It Doesn't Matter If You're from the Block or Not

Another girl who auditioned with me, whom the guys all flipped for, was a sexy Latina from the Bronx named Jennifer Lopez. Both of us made the cut. We were both struggling for money and trying to make it in the dance world, and even though we came from entirely different backgrounds, we became friends right then and there. She started coming down to the diner to get free food now and then, and we hung out and talked all the time. She heard about other auditions for other hip-hop artists, and before I knew it, I was dancing for Mary J. Blige, Salt-N-Pepa, New Kids on the Block, and all sorts of people. We both became friends with Darrin Henson, too, and it was clear that Puffy was driven and going places. We became fast friends. We all became friends. It was like I found my tribe.

More importantly, I found my *dance*. Even on the first day of the shoot, even though we were working with someone as talented as Darrin Henson, these people kept looking to *me* for ideas. They looked to the little things I was ad-libbing with my body. They looked to how I was moving and making things flow and pop in a way that was maybe a little more polished than what

was coming off the street. They took cues from my stance and the way I used the techniques of modern dance to string together the hip-hop moves.

Are you hearing what I'm saying? They took cues from *me*! Which means that hip-hop dance itself, this of-the-moment expression of music and style that was coming off the streets and starting to take over pop radio and MTV, was in the process of becoming something new—and I played a small role in creating what was happening!

I was helping shape the vision that was unfolding right in front of us, and I was discovering that I had more to give than just dancing; that my own vision, my own ideas about how a dance should look and flow, were worthy of others' attention.

So as the camera rolled, all I kept thinking was, *Whoa. This is* amazing. *This is* freedom. *This is* creative.

What I studied at Alvin Ailey was "contemporary" dance, but hip-hop was *truly* contemporary. It was new. It was fresh. And I quickly became a part of this group of people who were creating the sound, inventing and *reinventing* the genre and what it was all about, and they valued me and my moves and my opinions in the process.

And it all happened so fast! We started shooting the video just a few days after the audition, and it seemed like no time after that when the video was released. Start to finish. *Boom!*

It felt pretty cool. I was in a *video* now, dancing in ways I'd never danced before. In ways *no one* had ever danced before. I was smiling and shaking my tail feather exactly how I wanted to but was never before allowed to. And I was dancing in front of millions of people!

I was expressing my gift, living my dream, and discovering

more about what that dream really meant and the amazing feeling that came over me when I was *in it*.

Once I discovered the world of hip-hop, the feeling, the freedom, the joy I experienced in New York City went next level. Higher than anything I'd ever known. I was *dancing*, in the biggest sense of the word, as *described* by the Word.

Suddenly my obsession with becoming a part of the second company and aiming for the first company at Alvin Ailey fell to the wayside. Not because I didn't love it, and not because I wasn't good enough, but because of the new feeling I had. It was like seeing a brand-new road laid in front of me. That feeling—the very same feeling that I trusted when God took me from a seat in the O'Keefe Centre at twelve years old all the way to New York City—let me know that all I had to do now was put one foot in front of the other and follow wherever God was taking me. My dream was his gift, and only he knew its greatness. Only he knew where it would lead.

STEP 3

Train and Sustain

*Y*ou have *baseball hat* on," my ballet teacher said in her thick accent.

"Yeah," I replied. In fact, I'm pretty sure my baseball hat was on *backward*.

The freedom of hip-hop changed me in almost every way. After just one audition I was hooked—on all of it: the music, the movement, the look. It's like a whole new world opened up to me. And that made the rest of my fourth and fifth years at Alvin Ailey a little . . . complex. It wasn't long before I was dressing differently than my classmates and spending more time away from school. For whatever reason, on this particular day, I decided to push the envelope in ballet class.

My teacher stood there looking at me, and from the expression on her face you would've thought I'd just insulted her mother.

"What are you, trying to do ballet in that baseball hat?" she said, almost spitting her words.

"It's what I'm feeling," I said.

She threw me out.

I wasn't trying to be disrespectful. It was just a feeling. I was just trying to be *me*.

I couldn't help myself. I didn't want to quit Alvin Ailey. I just realized that the purpose of my time at Alvin Ailey might not be leading me to a destination of becoming an Alvin Ailey dancer. My destination might be something different. I identified more with the freedom, the liberation of hip-hop than with the idea of conforming to the vision of joining the second company—and that left me continuing school with one foot in and one foot out.

I was at this amazing turning point where I would've been ready to audition for and probably make the second company, but when I tried to explain to my mother what was happening, she was like, "You did all this training to wanna go do the hip-hop? Are you *crazy*? You wanna throw all that training away?"

"No, Mom," I said. "I'm not throwing it away. God just has more in store for me."

I still loved the training, but I was living out a *process*. I was hanging on to the dream as a *feeling*, not a concrete set of circumstances, and the feeling didn't stop at Alvin Ailey. The feeling told me I had the capacity to do more.

It was hard to keep a foot in both worlds. The Alvin Ailey world turned a cold shoulder to hip-hop. There was a massive amount of snobbery from "serious" dancers concerning anything that went on in the pop and hip-hop worlds.

My peers at school thought I was selling out. "Laurieann! You're doing hip-hop?" they asked.

Yes, I was. But you know what I was really doing? I was beginning to develop my own voice as a choreographer and visionary, which was a gift I didn't even know I had at the time.

Not every choreographer dances. Some are visionaries who can see the dance, who can string movement together even though they can't dance it themselves. And most dancers are not choreographers; they need somebody else's vision in order to bring out the gifts of their movement. I happened to have the skills to be both, and I was starting to put two and two together. I realized I could *see* the movement before I brought it to life, and I also understood the importance of putting *intention* behind the movement.

It's wild when I look back on it. I had no way of knowing that the steps I was taking were the very steps that would allow me to later create whole visual and movement worlds for Nicki Minaj and Missy Elliott and more, choreographing dances that would be simultaneously pedestrian *and* based in technique.

The choices I made then, just by following my feeling, would later allow me to choreograph Lady Gaga from a basis of what I call "Jazz 101," which was based in so much technique even though it was offbeat and simple. Or my Puff Daddy hip-hop, with timing that was inspired and influenced by a combination of tap dancers like Gregory Hines and the Nicholas Brothers, the ballet great Mikhail Baryshnikov, modern dance legend Katherine Dunham, and traditional African dances, infused into my style of hip-hop. My training would later allow me to string hip-hop dance moves together into a production, like a ballet or contemporary piece, so the choreography would have a sustainability that a street dancer or the dance of the week would not have. That would become my style: creating dances as if they were for theater, but for TV awards shows and on tours and in arenas.

Hip-hop but *modernized*; executed with a beginning, middle, and end. Hip-hop dance that would tell a whole story.

So I didn't reject the training. I didn't quit school. I just continued it with a different purpose: to further my own course, rather than to become an Alvin Ailey dancer.

If I hadn't valued the technique and skills I was learning at Alvin Ailey, I might have left before my training was over. I was conflicted—committed, but wanting more. So I went to Broadway Dance Center and Steps on B'way to get some jazz training outside of Ailey. I took classes from some of the best in the business, greats like Cecilia Marta (creator of an original style known as World Jazz) and Otis Sallid (who would conceive the Broadway show *Smokey Joe's Café*). In order to sustain myself financially while I did this training, I took a second job at the bagel stand right there at Steps on B'Way, which allowed me to take those classes for free. That training, in addition to my Ailey training, helped prepare me for everything that was coming next—including going on the road as a dancer for some of the biggest pop and hip-hop artists in the world.

I couldn't have known all of that as it unfolded. I just followed the feeling, and it turns out that the feeling was all I needed to follow in order for God to begin to fill my capacity.

The feeling of my dream told me I needed to train, so I trained. I found a way to sustain myself financially as I did, just as I'd found a way to sustain myself financially all through school. Making sure you sustain yourself on your journey is important— not only financially, but emotionally and spiritually too.

I was still waitressing, not because I wanted to be a waitress, but because I understood that waitressing was what I needed to do until I could sustain myself as a working dancer. When the opportunity came to go on tour with Mary J. Blige (which I'll tell you about in the next chapter), I left the diner.

Then I found ways to pay my bills as a *dancer* rather than take some other job. I went on every single audition I could possibly go on. I danced in videos, I danced at a bar mitzvah, I danced at corporate events and car shows. I danced wherever I could get paid to dance, and I never stopped. Once I left the diner, I never went back. And the only reason that happened is because I chose to train, and to *keep* training, in order to give myself the skills and technique that would set me apart and make me the best dancer I could be. That ability gave me a stability that would sustain my dream. My dancing could sustain me financially so I wouldn't have to go back to waitressing.

One thing led to the next, and the next. I couldn't skip the training if I wanted to sustain my dream.

These days, people on Instagram want to be like, "Oh, I took one class. I'm ready!" That is just not true. The value of training is that you can sustain the journey, the process, the evolution of your gift and your career and your dream.

It takes *work*. However difficult it is, as long as you remember your dream, the work you're doing—whatever work it is—is so you can receive *more*. If you find it taking more time than you wish it would, remember: It may be because you're meant to do something greater. You're meant to receive greater. It takes more time to train for greater things! So you have to be prepared for that.

Or maybe you're not training for more. Maybe you're training to be the best you can be at whatever you're choosing to do right now. That's up to you. If you're feeling happy and fulfilled in your career at this moment, then training can be all about sustaining the feeling you already have.

Maybe you have a capacity to be like a lady I met at the airport one day. She was cleaning the bathroom at JFK with a great big smile on her face. She took the time to hand people paper towels and to keep everything looking good. I asked her why she seemed so full of joy, and she told me she was happy to be there helping others.

Wow, I thought. *Hallelujah to that!* In her job, she was constantly gifted with the feeling of fulfillment, right where she was: in a bathroom at JFK. If that's your calling, then the beautiful thing about it is you never have to be in a place where you don't

The value of *Training*
is that you can sustain
the *journey*, the
process, the *evolution*
of your gift and your
career and your dream.

know if you're meant for something more in the eyes of everyone else. You can be happy, right where you are! If your capacity is full, and you *don't* have the appetite for more, that's okay.

I have an appetite to do what I do: to create, to dance, to envision, to lift my artists into being their best selves and to touch the world through them, over and over again.

We are our *own* center stage. We are our *own* spotlight.

Unfortunately, our vision of giving "behind the scenes" players the props they're due is broken. For example: This notion that "Those who can, *do*, and those who can't, *teach*" is one of the greatest lies we've ever been told. Teachers in their element, fulfilling their gifts to launch students into their own dreams and greatness, are a gift to the world! We should celebrate and compensate every one of them far more than we do.

In the entertainment world, the machine of the big business that drives what we see and buy was built for the creative geniuses to utilize, to further their art and vision in the world. But somewhere along the line we gave the machine too much power. It uses creative people instead of *us* using *it*. The machine makes the creators and the artists who aren't center stage seem like we're expendable. This is true in so many creative fields: in movies, in magazines, in publishing, in television. The machine takes the profits while the stars get the glory, and everybody else is left churning like cogs in the wheel, thinking their gifts aren't worthy—when they *are*! We just need to change our perspective, stand up in our God-given power, and recognize the worthiness in ourselves, so someday (maybe *this* day, in *this* season) we can change the power structure that devalues us.

Until that happens, I pray that more of us understand that what we have and what we're giving is *enough*. We should be proud of where we are on our own journeys, proud of expressing whatever bit of our gifts we are able to share in whatever roles we are currently in. And maybe, just maybe, we should turn to the artists and creative people around us and thank them, to let them know they are valued for the gifts they share with us.

If you *do* have the appetite for more, keep training and sustaining. As you do, more and more will come your way. Not only will God open the door to more opportunity to express your gifts, but he also will open your eyes to see more clearly.

Never Give Up

Sustaining myself financially at the diner was something I needed—for a season, during my first few years in New York. But leaving the diner was a big step in the right direction, as much for personal reasons as it was for my evolution toward becoming the choreographer and artist developer I would eventually be.

It turns out my time at the diner was also training me about love and relationships. I was learning to keep my eyes open, to be aware that not everything is always as it seems.

It turns out that the owner of the diner wasn't keeping our relationship from his family because of the color of my skin. He was keeping our relationship quiet because he was leading a double life. He had a whole other *life* back in New Jersey, which is where he lived—without me—whenever he wasn't at the diner or taking me on a trip somewhere. He was *married*. He had *kids*.

I was mortified. I felt like a fool. I cried more than I'd ever cried in my life.

But thank *God* he opened my eyes to the truth when he did. Because having my eyes opened allowed me to leave the security of the diner with no hesitation. There was nothing left to draw me back in. Nothing that would hold me down to the status quo of staying put in the place where I was.

It was time for me to move on—and I *did*.

Was I scared? Heck, yes! The tour with Mary J. Blige would last only a few weeks. I would make enough money to pay the bills for two or three months—and then what? I had no idea what would come next. No idea where my next paycheck would come from. That is scary! This is real life we're living, and there's rent to pay, food to buy, electric bills and phone bills that are due, emergencies that happen. If you're not making money, those things get real *real* fast.

Know what's bigger than the rent and the electric bills? God.

And God's expression is in *you*, in your dream. That never goes away. That *is* guaranteed. So we need to retrain ourselves to be sustained not by worldly expressions but by God's gifts.

When you're faced with a big change, a next step, or a force that seems to be turning negative on you, pushing you down, taking away what you've thought of as the success that you've reached so far—whether it's personal, in a relationship, in your career, or anywhere else—when that happens, you've got to turn internally to what you're called to be. To find life within you. To find the *source*.

What can reboot, what can outlast the negativity, what can outlast the doubt and fear is the dream, the passion, the purpose. What *sustains* you getting up and going back to the process of *becoming*.

The greats in sports, the motivational speakers, the business leaders in their business books, they all try to tell us, "Never give up."

But what does that *mean*?

Never giving up means that even if you're not feeling fully fulfilled, you keep going back to the *one thing* that drives you: the feeling of your dream. When you focus on that feeling, when you pour yourself into training the gifts that God gave you, the power of that feeling becomes stronger than anything that stands in your way or anything that might be getting you down.

If you do two things that fulfill your passion, that move you toward *becoming* in the face of whatever life throws at you, then as a matter of course, those two things will eventually become five things, and then *ten* things. You'll get to the point where you evolve into the fulfillment of yourself. And then? You're just *being*. You're not thinking about who you are; you're *being* who you are. You're not worried about tomorrow, because it's already a part of who you are *today*.

Never giving up means being that which will produce what you need to be tomorrow. Therefore, there's no anxiety. There's only the joy of living. In that joy, there is this space where we feel the surprise and the peace of realizing, *Oh, my! I've been sitting here painting for ten hours straight!* And we know that tomorrow is going to be all that we need it to be, because we gave today the very best of ourselves. We walked in the fulfillment of ourselves.

Training the muscle to sustain is not automatic. Every artist I've ever met has had to overcome at some point; to learn how to train and sustain; to learn how to never give up. Every one! Alicia Keys, Katy Perry, Lady Gaga, Nicki Minaj, even someone as seemingly confident as Puffy. So you are not alone in the struggle.

Never giving up means
that even if you're not
feeling fully fulfilled,
you keep going back
to the *one Thing* that
drives you: the *feeling*
of your dream.

Learning to trust in the gift of your dream takes training, and we have to go at it again and again, just like an athlete might train in the gym, year round, every day to get to a place where she's ready to go for one run, one lift, one lap, one jump. We have to train that muscle to the point where we go, "Whew. Okay. Well, I think that's all I've got for you today. Muscle's tired. We'll pick it up tomorrow."

I grew up in a house where boxing was the thing. My dad loved boxing, and we watched it on TV every night he could find a fight.

I think I fell in love with it because I am a fighter myself. Not a physical fighter; it's not the physical aspects that interest me so much. I love the discipline, the training, the dedication it takes for a fighter to enter the ring at his peak. I also love the strategy of the fight, because the goal is to knock something out, to get beyond something.

The strategy, the twist, the turn, the uppercut in my life has been for me to apply that mentality to every single situation that's tried to tell me I'm nothing. Every situation that's filled me with doubt. I want to be the heavyweight champion of my world.

The fight is to *become*. To maintain the dream, to stay in it. And as life works against that, you gotta block it, you gotta block it, you gotta block it, like a boxer would.

I still love watching boxing. I love watching Floyd Mayweather walk to the ring. I go back and watch all the old Muhammad Ali fights. I watch Sugar Ray Leonard. I watch Mike Tyson. I am obsessed with Laila Ali. I'm inspired by their physical discipline, yes, but I'm more inspired by the mental fight, the endurance that you need to withstand eight rounds, the will that has to kick in when you feel like you can't go another round. It's the will and the spirit of a boxer that I connect with, and everybody has that spirit. You were created with the will to *become.*

Whatever it takes to inspire that will to come out in you, to return to you—go watch it, listen to it, find it! You need that will to fight against the challenges that come, the Dreamkiller of a teacher who says your feet are too flat; the mornings when you're too tired to get up. You need that will to bounce back from every fall and keep fighting 'til the end.

The comeback, the training—it's all part of the process.

Muhammad Ali called himself "the greatest," and he *was.* He was the greatest boxer in the world in his time. But he was also much more. He became a civil rights leader and a fighter for peace in his stance against the Vietnam War. He gave back to children and wound up inspiring the whole world in his greatest fight—his battle against Parkinson's disease.

To actually become "the greatest" was a lifelong journey for Ali. We *all* have a journey in us, and we never know how far God will take us if we trust in him.

When we're taking steps to fulfill our dreams, we don't have to worry about tomorrow. We know we're going to be even *better* tomorrow. Tomorrow's about to be on and popping!

It seems like we, as a society, are consumed by worry and fear *all the time.* But we can live without worry and fear if we listen to what God gave us—because fear is just the absence of faith.

Pharmaceutical companies have convinced you that this drug will take care of worry and fear. Pushers and peers might tell you that this illegal substance will take care of worry and fear. Snake-oil salesmen will tell you that this drink or this exercise or this mantra or this device will eliminate your worry and fear. But what will *actually* take care of your worry and fear is the spiritual journey of becoming who God wants you to be. If you're doing that, on whatever level, in whatever capacity you're meant to be doing it, then your worry and fear slips away and you know you're going to be okay.

When you're pursuing your dream, "worry and fear" become the catalysts for "faith and hope."

And faith and hope can sustain you through anything.

In order to sustain, you need to train your mind to react in a new way—a way that supports you instead of one that gives your power away. All it takes is realizing that when you feel fear, it's really an opportunity to feel faith.

Faith is real. And you can define it however you want to define it, but when faith is there—even if all it amounts to is belief in your dream, your gift, your passion—then there is nothing to be fearful of. Instead, you turn to your faith and say, "Yes, faith! Let me know what's happening tomorrow, because I'm *in you* right now."

Unfortunately, we're not taught that fear is the flag that should trigger faith. We're not taught that worry is the opportunity to produce faith. I try to teach that to everybody I can, which is why I'm trying to share it with you right now.

The Bible tells us that "faith without works is dead" (James 2:26 KJV). That means it takes work to make your faith real. It takes the training of your mind as much as it takes the training of your body.

God promises, "I will never leave you nor forsake you" (Hebrews 13:5). When you feel fearful, you have to consciously train yourself to remember that truth. You have to trust God and remind yourself, *God told me to dance. He told me that this dream, this feeling, is his gift in me. Now that I'm faced with this change, this obstacle, this intrusion, this roadblock, this fork in the road, I don't know exactly what I'm going to do, but I know I'm going to hold on to the dream, hold on to his gift—and as long as I do, he will not forsake me.*

Stepping forward in faith in my own life, coming off my first major tour without a job or a paternal-type patron of a boyfriend to fall back on, the only things I could do were to pray and to go back to training. I had to stay focused on my dream.

And because I did that, one morning the phone rang: "Hi, Laurieann. We have an audition for you!"

I was able to keep moving forward.

Ask any artist who has stayed the course, and similar stories will surface.

They may have been broke, they may have been down to nothing, they may have been scared they weren't going to make it—but then one day, as long as they kept working at it, and as long as they kept the faith, the call came.

When it happens, when all that "keeping the faith" and "training and sustaining" pays off, even in a small way, it strengthens the muscle of perseverance. Eventually you get into an alignment with the process of becoming the person you have always been designed to be.

When that happens, you start to create the flow that best fits you. The dance, as I call it. Your rhythm. Your eight-count. And you start to choreograph and understand the way you dance, the way you sing, the way you move. There are up times, there are down times, there are high times, there are low times, there are fast times, there are slow times. As you train and sustain, through all that experience you gain an understanding that what comes in and out of your dance either enhances it or is a signal to move in a different rhythm away from it. *Oh, what is that? Aha! I recognize that. I'd better two-step* away *from that beat.*

You don't worry about it. You just deal with it. You trust in it. You know you'll be all right.

Just to be clear: having faith in your gift doesn't mean you get to just sit by the phone and wait for the audition or the sale or the promotion or the screen test to come in. You have to do the work.

Too many people think, *Okay, I've got faith, and that's all I need!* Then they sit there twiddling their thumbs, waiting for an opportunity, waiting for God to do all the work. That's not how it works. This is *your* life, *your* gift, *your* dream to pursue. You've got a capacity to fill, and you've got to go out and fulfill it.

You can't rely on confirmation from others to get you through, either. It has to come from within.

Even as a young kid, when I was being told I couldn't be a ballerina, I relied on the affirmation of the feeling along the way. I could not lie about how I felt when I danced; or later, how I felt when I got a job dancing; or later still, how I felt when I was able to choreograph, and create, and direct, and develop artists. When I was doing it, I could not lie to myself that I wasn't in the best possible place for me, that I wasn't working at my optimum capacity. I felt *energized.* I got lost in it. The joy I felt in being immersed in my gift and in my passion was totally enough for me. That's why even though most jobs in my early days as a dancer lasted only six or eight weeks, I rarely worried about what would happen after that, because all I knew was for the next little bit I had a *gig.* I was living my dream. I was *becoming.* And God would sustain me when nothing else could.

In those early days I might not necessarily have defined my

belief as faith, or even having to do with God, but even then, I couldn't deny that what I was doing felt *right*.

Now? I know it is God. He called me to this—not only to my career but to this book itself—so I can share this with you. In my own faith, I know this to be true: God is the master choreographer. He is the one designing your dance. You are his dancer. So dance as he has called you to dance! Do the rhythm that he gave you to do!

When you tap into *that*, when you trust in *that*, when you develop the faith to believe in him and the dream he has given you, you become full of hope and excitement for what comes next. You'll feel, as I feel, "I can't wait to see how he finishes this piece!"

STEP 4

Stay in Your Yes

*N*ot long after the Heavy D video hit, I landed an audition for the singer Bobby Brown.

Bobby had broken out big-time from his days with the R&B boy band New Edition, and he was about to head out on a solo headlining tour, playing giant arenas all over the country. I was *ready*. I knew it. I felt it in my bones. I went to that audition all fired up—and he liked me! He offered me the tour. Can you imagine getting that kind of work right out the gate like that? I hadn't even graduated from dance school.

But I left that audition not *wanting* to dance for Bobby Brown. After I danced for him, he looked at me sort of leeringly. He was looking me up and down in this sexually forward kind of way, and that set off red flags for me.

I wasn't a promiscuous person. At the time, men in hip-hop were known to be aggressive, and the atmosphere was misogynistic. I was scared of that. I was young, just a *baby* still. I'd heard about things like this happening, but it had never happened to me before. So I got out of there as fast as I could.

One of Bobby's dancers, a girl named Leslie "Big Lez" Segar, was the coolest girl in the street in hip-hop dance. I told her what happened, and she was like, "Well, you should dance for my girl Mary J. Blige instead."

I didn't know who Mary J. Blige was, but I said, "I'll do anything, 'cause I'm not comfortable going on tour with you guys."

"Okay," she said. "Well, Mary's going to be opening for Bobby, so you'll still get to tour the big venues."

Wow! That's perfect, I thought.

Big Lez brought me in, and when I met Mary, she was just the coolest person ever. We connected instantly. I opted to take the opening-act job not just because I felt safer working for a female artist but because we made a bond. I didn't care that I was missing out on the headlining gig, even though that would have been a giant leap up for my career—and would have paid a lot more. I had to trust that my feelings were guiding me in the right direction.

The opening act was fine because it gave me the feeling I was looking for. The headlining act gave me a different feeling—a feeling of danger, of being out of control. Something about it wasn't lining up.

There wasn't a #MeToo movement in those days. Not even close. In fact, there were other dancers who told me that I should do whatever I needed to do to get ahead. It was kind of accepted that girls in our world would hook up with the men of hip-hop, because those men held the power to make or break any one of us.

I refused. Not just with Bobby, but at other points in my career, with other men. And there are people who would say I hurt my career because of that.

Well, guess what? I might have slowed down how fast my career as a dancer was progressing, but know what I didn't hurt? My dream. My heart. My soul.

I'll take that choice anytime, anywhere.

How could I have sustained myself in the pursuit of my dream if I wasn't true to myself in those moments?

It cost me jobs. It cost me paychecks. It cost me socially, too, because I wasn't one of the "cool kids." But I'm secure in the knowledge that the jobs I got came from my talent, my drive, my work ethic, and my skills—and *nothing else.*

I think it was worth it, and I hope you do too.

It got a little lonely sometimes, feeling like I wasn't "in" with the guys at the top of the chain or the girls who were willing to make those sorts of compromises. I didn't have anyone around me to tell me I was making the right decision. I wasn't going to church. My mom was in the process of moving back to Jamaica. My sisters were living in Canada. Who could I talk to about something as sensitive as this? The only one I could talk to was God, in my own conversation with myself, by aligning myself with what God had called me to do.

I didn't align with a particular faith at that time. The only reason I knew what to do in response to those situations was because I recognized, *That's not in line with the feeling of my dream.*

I was following the path of *becoming.* When the dancers around you are going places faster than you are, it's hard to stay true to the idea that this process is okay, because there's something *greater* for you. But that's exactly what I want to tell you, especially if you're questioning the way to move ahead in whatever line of work you're in. Please listen to your feeling! Does what you're being asked to do align with the good feeling you get when you're chasing your dream? If so, then say yes. That good feeling is your yes!

And if it doesn't align with that good feeling, then it's not good for you. It's just not.

It's sometimes hard to see it when you're in it, especially when you know that other people are getting ahead while you're staying patient and true to who you are at your core. But someday, just as I have, you will look back and see how the path makes sense. You'll see why the choices you made were stronger and more powerful in the end. It's all about trusting God and the path he's laying out for you.

As we now fully recognize, this kind of inappropriate behavior happens in all professions. I also believe that sometimes the dream is so beautiful that when you're in it, when you're achieving it, the Devil is attracted to it. That's where he gives you a choice, dangling your desire and your passion right in front of you—the shortcut to get to your dream.

The second you choose the shortcut, you lose.

As long as I followed the feeling of my dream, saying no was easy, because no one ever got to me and presented an idea that was better than the vision that God had given me. Some people talk about the vision as if it's something you can see, but my vision was always based on a *feeling*. And that feeling ran deeper than anything my eyes could perceive.

That is why, from the very beginning of this book, I have said, "I want to speak to your dream. I want to speak to the feeling you have."

I want to speak to the feeling that comes while you're planting flowers, when you're fully conscious in understanding that it's the best feeling in the world, and you're like, *I'm* free *when I do this. I'm happy. I'm* me!

I want to speak to that thing you feel when whatever you're doing makes you feel good, like you can do it all day long without growing tired. When you're doing it or even *thinking* about it, you're not thinking of anything else.

What *is* that in you—the one thing that will get you to roll out of bed in the morning, excited to go, with no hesitation, no dread, just love and excitement and passion?

That's *magic*. That's your yes.

It can be something you haven't done for a really long time. It can be more than one thing. It can also evolve, just as it evolved for me.

Once we establish (or reestablish) the muscle that understands how to *choose* that feeling—or surrender to that feeling automatically—then we're on our way to greatness. We're on our way to God's glory. Because that feeling from our dream, which is God's gift inside each of us, is capable of sustaining us and carrying us through *anything.*

The feeling of our dream will drive us down the path that God lays out before us.

Dodging Distractions

In the middle of that expansive time, as I began to step out into the professional world at the same time I was finishing my training at Alvin Ailey, I made one of my biggest mistakes.

I was given the opportunity of a lifetime: I got hired to be part of the skeleton crew for a movie directed by Spike Lee called *Malcolm X*, which starred Denzel Washington as the revolutionary civil rights leader.

I would be part of the stand-in dance crew that helps a choreographer and director bring a big dance scene to life in a movie. Our team would work out the movements while the crew worked out the camera placement and lighting to the point of perfection, so there'd be no wasted time when film was rolling and the multimillion-dollar actors were on set.

The scene I was hired for was in the opening of the film, as Denzel walks into a jazz club to the sound of "Stompin' at the Savoy." It was like a modern twist on musical numbers from the golden age of Hollywood, and it was choreographed by none other than the great Otis Sallid, with whom I'd been training. Otis was like a male Debbie Allen, just a huge figure in the dance world. And this film was the talk of the city. This was Spike Lee's chance to emerge from his status as an acclaimed indie director into the big-time Hollywood world of the Scorseses and Spielbergs. It was a big-budget film of historical importance, so every member of the cast and crew was at the top of his or her game. Even the skeleton crew was full of renowned dancers, full-time professionals, the best of the best.

I auditioned in front of Otis and Spike Lee himself and booked the gig. This was truly my big break. A chance to move up in the dance world, not by a step or two, but by leaps and bounds. Just to be in the same room as those dancers meant the world to me. (Not to mention that it was a union gig, a real paycheck, which I desperately needed at that moment!)

My dream of becoming a professional dancer was being fulfilled, at the highest level, sooner than I ever imagined possible. Sooner than anyone else imagined possible, too, including a friend of mine. She was a triple threat—a singer/dancer/actor—and she could not *believe* I got that part.

I came home after our first few rehearsals just glowing. Truly *shining*. I told her how professional everybody was, and how Otis told us that very day, "Do not show up late on this set or you will be locked outside. No excuses. We're heading into production in two days. If you're late, you're fired. Got it?" She and I laughed, like, *Who would ever show up late to a dream gig like that?*

I told her all about the dancers I'd met, and the energy they had, and the intricacy of the choreography with what felt like a thousand different moving parts to it, and the fact that Otis put *me*, the youngest and least-experienced dancer in the place, into the role of a featured dancer who would pop out right between Denzel's legs when they filmed the actual scene!

"Girl, come *on*! We gotta go to the China Club tonight and celebrate," she said.

The China Club was *the* hot spot in New York at that time, the place where all the stars went. The kind of place where you either had to know somebody to get past the bouncers, or had to look like the kind of girl the stars on the inside might want to meet.

It was a see-and-be-seen *scene*.

I wasn't even into clubs like that. I was too busy rehearsing and practicing and staying in my process to care about wasting money on drinking at some club. But she seemed so happy for me, and she insisted that we needed to go.

I didn't want to let her down. So I went.

I'm not sure what happened after that, but I think there were shots involved. All I know is that I woke up late the next day.

I woke up after I was already supposed to be on set.

I was frantic.

I threw on whatever clothes were lying on my floor and *ran* to the subway. I just made the train as the doors were shutting, and I was on the train when Otis Sallid called me on my cell phone. The great Otis Sallid was calling *me*, and I was under the ground with the phone cutting in and out. I couldn't hear what he said. He couldn't hear me. The train was rocking and the world was spinning, and the call dropped.

I couldn't understand what had happened. I couldn't understand why I'd done this. I didn't have the bandwidth to understand that I'd been duped by a jealous "friend" who wanted me to fail. That sorry fact wouldn't sink in until later.

When I reached my stop, I ran to the top of the stairs and called Otis back. He picked up the phone, and all he said to me was "Laurieann, don't bother coming."

Click.

Do you wanna know what devastation is?

Of course I still went. I ran all the way to the set, hoping and *praying* that he'd give me another chance. But the doors were locked when I got there. I had no choice but to wait outside. I waited and waited until everybody filed out on their lunch break. I caught the eyes of some of those professional dancers I was just getting to know—and they shook their heads in disappointment at me.

I finally stepped in, and Otis took one look at me and shook his head with the most disappointment of all. He didn't throw me out right away. He patiently let me stand there and plead my case. I *begged* him to let me come back and I *swore* it would never happen again. And he said, "No, kid. I can't do it. You heard what I said yesterday. You were late. You're fired."

I walked home crying and cried all night long. I ran over everything in my head, second-guessing myself, kicking myself, beating myself up for not turning my "friend" down. If I'd been listening to my truth, if I'd been focused on my dream, I should've heard what she asked of me and been like, "Nope, I can't go to the China Club, girl. I got a job!" I should've thrown it right back at her. Instead, I wanted to make *her* feel comfortable—maybe because I didn't think I was deserving enough.

All night long I kept asking, *Why would God let that happen to me? Why would God give me that chance and let me ruin it?* And today, I know: God allowed it because I had a lesson to learn.

Going to the club, the drinking, the celebrating—maybe there's a season for that, but it is certainly not when you're just starting out, when you're first catching your break and discovering the power of your dream in action.

Success was looking me in my face, and I wasn't ready for it yet. I wasn't trained to understand, *This is* your *road, this is not* her *road; this is your shot, not hers. You're so busy trying to make sure you're nice to everybody that when someone suggested something that didn't belong in your process, you didn't know how to deflect it. You need to learn how to deflect it, Laurieann!*

Even if that girl hadn't purposefully tried to hurt my chances out of jealousy, there might have been some other person or longing or feeling that came along and tempted me to go to the club and get distracted by the trappings of success.

Did you ever stop and think about that phrase: *the trappings of success?*

The clubs, the cars, the money, the champagne—we glamorize the trappings of success. But they're traps! They're not the success itself. Why do we glamorize the trappings when what we really ought to glamorize is the *purpose?*

I don't want to see you in the club pouring champagne on somebody. That is what society tells you is fame and fortune, but that image is desensitizing, numbing, distracting you from your purpose.

That feeling you get when you're up onstage under the spotlight or in your studio working out the kinks, perfecting your gifts—*that's* where the high is. That's where the power is. That's where the glory is: in doing the things we are gifted by God with the ability to do as human beings.

That is where your yes should be.

The flow that we're talking about—the feeling of not having to come down from that high because the high is you being in your purpose and your passion—try *that* on for size. Imagine feeling that power, feeling that good about your life. And imagine feeling that high because you're just doing it. You're living your passion. You're pursuing what matters to you, what feels right to you, your purpose—and you're sticking to it.

The clubs and parties are alluring. They're sexy. You might not feel sexy right now, alone in your room, practicing your gift. Other people might not think it's sexy, either. They'll call you out and try to pull you away from your personal place of happiness, and you might think you need that attention in order to feel better. I want to tell you that you don't need the celebrity and excitement. You are living a *good life*.

Especially in the music world, there seems to be this misconception that the party is the purpose, as if you've only "made it" when you're dripping in diamonds and champagne and surrounded by beautiful people. And then people want to skip to that, as if it doesn't matter what it takes to get there.

No. Those are the trappings. Those are not the success.

The trappings fade. They go away. But the purpose doesn't. The dream doesn't. The truth doesn't.

Say yes to *that*.

That *feeling* you get
when you're up onstage
under the spotlight or in
your studio working out
the kinks, *perfecting*
your gifts—that's
where the high is. . . .
That is where your
yes should be.

Stay on Your Path

Remember how my mom would always keep me waiting at the end of my long dance-class days on Saturdays when I was little? How I'd wind up tap-dancing in the parking lot just waiting for her to show up, and how she'd bring me a sugar doughnut to appease me when she finally did?

That taught me patience.

I'm sure glad my mom taught me patience when I was young, because I would spend pretty much the entirety of the 1990s paying my dues. I was working hard, training and sustaining, struggling at times, watching as some people rose to what we tend to think of as the top, while I was still barely making my rent. It's hard to accept that you're doing things right when you see that happening all around you. But we're all on different timelines. We all dance to our own beats. We all move at different speeds. The only way I was able to get through it all was by learning to say yes to my truth and no to the distractions and offers that didn't align with who I was—again and again and again and again.

I'm not sure why God felt the need to test me as much as he did or why I came so close to saying yes to things that didn't align with my truth quite as often as I did. I like to think that I went through all of those ups and downs in order to learn in a way that I would be able to share with up-and-coming artists later on— and share with you right here in this book. To me, that makes it all seem worthwhile.

Whenever I was tempted, whenever I was distracted, whenever I grew impatient, I ultimately chose my truth—to stay in alignment with my dream. I didn't give in, and I was *rewarded* for it. Like this one time I wound up between jobs, flat broke, and the rent was due.

I was living in an apartment on 44th and Tenth, in a neighborhood called Hell's Kitchen—maybe because for so many years it was where a lot of lower-income people and Irish-mob types lived (as portrayed in so many movies), or maybe because it's where the Devil cooks up all kinds of trouble.

It's a nice neighborhood today. In fact, ten years later I would move into a luxury building on 44th and Eleventh called (ironically enough) the Victory. It's one of the nicest buildings I've ever lived in. Funny how the world can change like that. But back in the 1990s, Hell's Kitchen was still rough.

I'd been taking hip-hop gigs for one-off appearances and small tours. I was just getting by. But for some reason, at this particular moment, the phone wasn't ringing. My rent was due. I didn't have the money to pay it, and I didn't have another gig in sight.

I mentioned this to my friend Larry, a really nice guy who was working as a dancer of a different sort in this same part of town, and he told me, "Hey, you know what? They're looking for waitresses at New York Dolls. They're hiring on the spot. You should go over there."

I felt desperate, like I *needed* to get hired on the spot. So I went.

New York Dolls was a popular "gentlemen's club."

A strip club.

The guy at the counter looked me up and down and said, "You want to dance?"

"No, no, no," I said. "No judgment, but that's not for me. Waitressing is just fine."

"You'll make a lot more money dancing," he said.

"No, that's okay."

"All right," he said. "You're hired."

I made pretty good tips waitressing that night, but I kept looking at these strippers getting all this money. The money was like rain. Green bills *everywhere*. They'd scoop it up off the stage by the armful at the end of every dance. It was crazy!

I went into the dressing room at the end of the night and this one girl was counting *thousands* of dollars. As for me, I'd done well at the tables. It was busy, and I'd made a little over $200. I could work with that. I figured I could give it to the landlord and keep working like this and tell him I'd get him all the rent that was due in a week or two. (I mean, I had to eat too!)

Back in my apartment that night, I couldn't stop thinking about the thousands of dollars in that dressing room.

And I got the temptation: *Maybe I* should *dance.*

I stood up and got buck naked in front of my full-length mirror—the mirror I'd bought at Walgreens drug store and leaned up against my wall, next to my futon that was still on the floor, and the milk crates I'd been using as a dresser ever since I first got a job at the diner—and I kept thinking about all that money. I *needed* that money. I wanted that money. Some part of me tried to convince myself that if I worked as a stripper, I would still be a "dancer," as if that made it okay. As if *that* was still in line with my dream.

I spun around, watching my naked body in the streetlight streaming through the window in that one-bedroom apartment, trying all these sexy moves, imagining moving like that in front of strange men, imagining what that would feel like. No matter how hard I tried to convince myself that the money would be worth it, my heart cried out, *I can't! I can't do this. No matter how much my rent is due, I can't do this.*

A little voice in my heart said, *Laurieann, if you do this, you will become a different version of yourself. I don't think you wanna know that person.*

I wasn't judging anybody. I think all kinds of people have their own reasons for going down that road. I didn't think less of my friend Larry for doing it. But this was *my* road, and I needed to stay on it, no matter how broke I was.

I had to trust in my dream. I had to trust in my faith. I had to stay in my yes.

Everything I had been through taught me to believe in the feeling that's *good*, in the feeling that I'm *okay with.*

I was solid enough in the feeling of my dream to know, *I'm not okay with this. This doesn't make me feel that joy. It feels weird. I feel uncomfortable.*

So I stopped. I said no.

I put on my sweats and climbed under the covers on my futon, knowing that I'd never be a stripper. *Ever.*

The very next morning, I got a call from Big Lez: "Hey, sis. This artist, Aaron Hall, who used to be in the group Guy—he's dropping a new single and he's performing at the Apollo. We're gonna be rehearsing for like possibly two weeks. Can you do it?"

"I sure can, Lez," I said. "I'll be there tomorrow."

That one gig was enough to pay for everything I needed.

I stayed in my yes in the face of a test, and *the very next morning*, God provided.

I ran into my friend Larry a couple of days later. He said, "You good, L?"

"Yeah, Larry," I said. "I got a job. I'm good. Thanks for the one day."

He was like, "No problem."

And—I wanna cry when I think about this—I never, *ever* had to do that again.

That situation could have turned into something else had I not had the faith. Had I not trusted my passion, my instinct, the voice of God in me that said, *Baby, this is not for you!*

It is so important to connect with that road map that God provides, with those little bread crumbs, with that sparkly-sparkly of the feelings and instincts we are blessed to have. And we can't get discouraged just because other people's roads seem to be taking them places faster than our own roads do.

Right after I finished my training at Alvin Ailey, I wound up going on tour as a dancer with a rapper named Candyman. Jennifer Lopez was on that tour too. We were roomies. We were so close. Back then we did everything together, including auditioning for a spot as a Fly Girl on this hot new black comedy show called *In Living Color*, which was created by Keenen Ivory Wayans.

Jen got cast. I didn't. Suddenly she was on TV, on this really hot show. She moved to LA and started down her own unique road toward celebrity and stardom.

I remember one time when we were hanging out at the diner, talking about auditions and how she was singing and really trying to be an actor. She wondered why I was still just doing dance auditions. "You'll never get famous being a dancer," she said.

She probably doesn't even remember saying this to me, because she said it in passing, like it was no big deal. But it stung. I don't think she meant that I, personally, would never make it as a dancer. I think what she meant was that dancers don't achieve the sort of global level of fame she was looking for—and, it turns out, she was destined to achieve. So I didn't let it discourage me. It was no different from Mr. Christopher telling me I would never be a ballerina, because I didn't look like his version of a ballerina. I hung on to *my* dream. I was living in *my* greatness, and looking to achieve *my* success.

Was I disappointed that I didn't get to be a Fly Girl? Yes! I was happy for Jen but disappointed for me. Apparently, the show was going for more sex appeal than I had at that time, and I didn't look the way they wanted a Fly Girl to look.

But guess what? Two years later, I went out for that gig again—and I got it.

For me, someone who oozed a different type of sexuality when she walked in a room, who wasn't comfortable with showing a lot of skin, it took some time to realize that my *confidence* was sexy. I could be okay with expressing it because it wasn't overt, it wasn't stripping, and it wasn't something that wound up revealing what was intimate and personal to me in terms of sexuality; it was intentionally expressing the concept of "sexiness" through the art form of dance.

Intention is *everything*.

Years later, I ran into Keenen at the World Music Awards in Monte Carlo, where I was choreographing the rapper Mase, and we spoke about it. Keenen said to me, "You know, you *weren't* sexy enough at first. You were *young*!" But he loved that I came back and auditioned again, and loved seeing how much I'd changed. What he didn't realize, and what I explained to him all those years later, is that it wasn't a *physical* change he saw in me; it was an acceptance of my confidence.

"Wow! That's amazing," he said.

Saying Yes To What's Next

My time as a Fly Girl didn't last long. Through Puffy, I connected with Missy Elliott, and instead of just dancing for her, I did her choreography. That led to my becoming a choreographer for Bad Boy Records and then Motown Records—these labels with so much energy and excitement, who worked with the best artists in the business. I went back to Mary J. Blige in this period and became the choreographer for her first headlining tour—and I got paid something like $40,000 for that gig! I was flying high until I heard that my old friend Jennifer Lopez had just booked the lead in a movie—for *millions*.

It's hard not to react when you encounter economic disparity like that. But I knew who I was. I wasn't J.Lo. That wasn't my lane. I struggled with reconciling the difference in paychecks, but I trusted in God's path for *me*.

What kept me going was my growing vision for choreography. With every passing week, that vision felt bigger and bigger in scope. I kept picturing what to me looked like masterpieces. A more fully polished vision of my dream.

In fact, I pitched one of my big ideas to Puffy, specifically for Mary J. Blige.

It was a whole theatrical, gangster-type concept—a whole gangster *movie*—based in ragtime, the Lindy, the energy of the Roaring Twenties, and the musicals of the 1940s, with men dressed in double-breasted suits.

I loved tap dance and was obsessed with Gregory Hines. The rhythms in tap matched the rhythm of hip-hop, and no one else seemed to notice this but me. *No one* had touched it. Hip-hop hadn't seen that fusion of the Nicholas Brothers meets hip-hop, you know?

I went into Puff Daddy's office. Everything was blowing up around him in the best way possible—he was huge at that point— and I was still nothing but a dancer/choreographer. I pitched him this grand idea with every bit of passion I had—and he laughed.

I don't think he had the ability to see it. He had never danced a jive. He didn't tap. He couldn't connect with everything I was talking about. It's not like I was pitching the Cotton Club to someone who was there, you know? I remember feeling this crushing blow, because I was so fired up about this vision for this dance and how it would elevate hip-hop to the next level. I thought, *How can he not see it? This is perfect for where we are with "Real Love" and the* My Life *album. This would kill onstage at the Soul Train Awards!*

"Nah," he said. "It's not street enough."

I left feeling crushed—but not for long. I was tapping more and more into this idea that no just meant a different yes for me. It was a no to Puffy, but that didn't change my vision or the excitement I had when I pictured that dance unfolding onstage.

I finally concluded, *All right, well, this vision must be for another artist. I'm just going to keep saying yes to the vision, and keep adding new things to it, and build it and build it until the time is right and the alignment is right.*

I didn't quit. I kept working for Mary. I didn't stop pitching ideas. I turned my attention to new ideas, and I built dances for Mary that fit her and fit what Puffy and the rest wanted for her in that moment. But I didn't let it go. I knew I was onto something, and that something would come in time. (Watch for more about this in the next chapter!)

I did what was good for *me* in that moment, even if it was only an internal thought process in support of my own vision.

It's so important to recognize and to support and to act in your own interests, even when the rest of the world doesn't align with them, especially when the chips are down.

It's so important to be able to say, *I don't know how I'm gonna pay this rent, God, but you're telling me this strip club is not for me. This vision I have for this piece of choreography isn't gonna work out right now, but I'm gonna choose me over the situation. I'm gonna choose my joy over the circumstances.*

It's not easy! At times, it's pure warfare. Especially when you're in those circumstances where you can't see it and you have to *believe* in it; when you can't see the solution, but you have to trust the feeling.

The world sells us this idea that if you're doing things right, your life is supposed to unfold perfectly. What does that even mean? That's not how it works. Life is full of challenges, temptations, distractions, and crossroads, all aimed at taking you away from your dream. These obstacles try to get you to align yourself with a false sense of gratification that empowers a limited version of yourself, not your *actual* self. When you're doing things right, you're staying in your yes; you're saying no to what's wrong for you; you're facing challenges with faith.

After even one month of stripping, I could have moved into a nice apartment, bought some real furniture and some fancy clothes, taken my friends out to dinner—treated myself as well as I believed I ought to be treated someday. How is that shortcut not super sexy and alluring?

Drugs offer something alluring, too: a shortcut to a high, a sensation of fulfillment, an immediate removal of worry and fear.

When people take these shortcuts, I believe that they (and the Devil, for that matter) are trying to mimic the feeling of what already belongs to us *without* the drugs, *without* selling out. But here's the deal: I think that when we endure, when we have the patience to stay true to our gifts and to being our full selves over the long haul, it feels like that—but it's permanent. It's not quick. It's not fleeting. It's accessible to all, and there are no downsides!

If only more of us had the knowledge of that.

That's not to say that worldly pleasures can't be ours too. God wants us to live with life's abundance: the joy and the celebration and the art and the parties and the fashion and the expression of you in your fullest self are all God-given! But I believe that people taint it all by taking shortcuts to get around what they think they don't want, which is the patience to understand God's way. We accept a false version instead. The Devil offers up false substitutions to lure us away from what takes time: the process of *becoming*. The Devil wants to get us to self-destruct before we have an opportunity to know who we really are—and to know the type of euphoria that doesn't require any drugs.

You don't need the fake version of it. You don't *want* the shortcut version of it. Because it's *nothing* like the real high you get when you're in your element and you're loving life and you're feeling the energy that comes when you're creating whatever it is you create.

If you don't feel like you're there yet, that's okay! It's a process.

To review a bit of what we covered in the first few chapters: The experiences you've had so far have enriched you in ways that you may not even understand. That job you're in that you don't like might be teaching you something that you need, something that will feed you and nurture you and sustain you later on. It's all training! And it's all good.

Wherever you are now, you're still in your process of *becoming*, because of the greatness you have to fulfill, right? Once you know that, once you're aware that you've been on this journey and there's still an evolution to come or an appetite that you haven't filled—instead of feeling negative about it, feel *empowered* by it. Think, *I'm not full yet. I still want more!*

The world says that's wrong. The world tells you, "Stop being a dreamer. Be grateful you've got what you got. Get your 401(k). Prepare for your future. Prepare for your retirement." I've got nothing against planning for your financial security, but is that all there is? Are the people you know who spend their time and effort preparing for retirement happy? I guarantee you the answer is no. There are benefits to thinking long term, of course, but it's a worldly process that doesn't have to define you. If you want to follow the worldly rules, go ahead—but at least find a balance with pursuing your dream. If you are a little afraid of that, remind yourself to choose faith over fear.

Keep pressing. Keep pushing. Keep persevering. Because then you will have progress, and then your performance will be perfected.

That's a lot of *P*s! But if you embrace those *P*s, then your version of *you* doesn't stop. And in time—in *your* time—you become greatness.

At this point in my career, after decades of ups and downs, I'm in a place where Puff is calling me, MTV is calling me, *So You Think You Can Dance* is calling me, parents and managers and A&R reps for up-and-coming artists and established artists who are looking for comebacks are calling me. My gifts are more in demand than ever.

By the world's standards, and especially by Hollywood's standards, I'm over-the-hill. I'm not the "hot young thang." On paper, you wouldn't think I would be so in demand.

But I am, because I haven't been operating on the world's standards.

I've been working more than half my life now to live up to *God's* standards—for *me*.

I'm living my best life today—and *that's* what I want to inspire. I want you to say yes to that! Not so you can get to a place of notoriety and fame, but so you can live your best life, whatever that means for *you*.

I am blessed to work in the entertainment business, with all of its pitfalls and temptations. I am able to work in this world, and create in this world, and sustain and evolve in this world, in a way that I don't believe I ever could without God in my life.

And that's why I want to share my personal story of transition—of *evolution*—with you next.

STEP 5

Dance Your Truth

By the mid-1990s, people all over the music industry were starting to notice my work and to know my name. I was now fully immersed in the dance and music industry. I was on tour with Mary. I had choreographed Missy. I was at Bad Boy Records, not only working as a choreographer for various artists but also sharing more of my vision as a creative director in artist development.

Before I knew it, some fine folks over at Motown Records invited me to work on a video for one of their artists. In that process, I met a producer named Mario Winans, a member of the talented Winans family. There was something about our energy, our chemistry, and instantly we fell for each other.

I remember saying to him early on, "You want to be over here with Bad Boy and all this *energy*." I was so excited by the music and the whole world that Puffy and everyone was creating in New York City, and I wanted Mario to be a part of all that.

"But you need to be careful," I warned him. "You need to remain *yourself*. Because it's dangerous."

I didn't even know why I said that to him. I barely knew him. But I knew that the party scene at Bad Boy was something different from what I wanted to be a part of. I worked around it but kept myself away from it—I was *in* that world but not *of* that world—and, like I said, that cost me socially. But I also sensed there were other things going on behind the scenes in the hip-hop record business too. Fights involving money and drugs and territory and gangs. Rivalries between the East Coast and West Coast rappers. I didn't know any details; I just knew it was there, and I liked Mario so much I didn't want him to get mixed up in any of that when he brought his talent over to Bad Boy's studios.

Anyway, we started dating. One weekend I went home with him to Detroit to meet his mother, Miss Vickie Winans. From the moment we met, she was everything to me.

She took us to church—Pastor Iona Locke's church—and the bishop was speaking that day. He had us all standing up as he spoke. Then he said, "If you're *not* lying to God, sit down."

That phrase stirred something in my spirit, in my soul. I hadn't gone to church in quite a few years, and I thought, *I couldn't ever have so much hubris as to think I'm* not *lying to God.* So I stood there—and I quickly realized I was the only person standing in the whole church.

It was my time.

With no warning, no warm-up, no preparation, the Holy Spirit was calling me to give my life to Christ.

All I remember is Vickie Winans putting her hand on my back, and then the Holy Spirit took over.

I was saved. I was born again, which is just a way to say that, in my heart and soul, I fully gave myself over to Jesus; I consciously, from the deepest place within myself, recognized him as my Lord and Savior. I devoted myself to him, openly, in a way I had never done before. I was filled up with the feeling and the knowledge that through him I am given eternal life.

I know this doesn't make sense to everyone, and I know people experience faith and God in all sorts of different ways. This is mine—my personal affirmation of my personal relationship with God.

I was *always* his. He had always been there, speaking to me through my dream, carrying me through every temptation—but there was that duration where he allowed me to experience my young adult years without being saved, I believe, in order to testify to the difference of life without him and life with his covering. Because from that moment on, I could truly understand what was worldly versus what was his. And from that day forward, God showed me who he was and wanted to be through me, which also meant showing me what no longer served me or my dream.

Back in New York, my relationship with Mario went off the rails. It fell into shambles. He got caught up in the partying scene with the Bad Boy crew and became someone I didn't even recognize. I had fallen for this man and his family, and he had brought me to Detroit where I was saved. I thought we were gonna get married! But he left me alone and brokenhearted in New York City.

It got dark.

I thought giving my life over to Christ would mean things would get better. But that wasn't how it worked.

I won't go into all the details here, because they're personal to me. As humans, we sometimes get backed into corners and try all the wrong things to get out of them. I was definitely in danger of doing that. Once again, the Devil came gunning for me.

Finally one night, after weeks of despair, I was in my apartment at 44 Wall Street, in the shadows of the Twin Towers in Lower Manhattan, and out of nowhere I felt what I can only describe as some sort of demonic attack in my kitchen. I was scared. I can't explain it. It felt like my apartment was *haunted*.

I tried to go to bed, to shut it out, but I couldn't sleep. I was so scared that I couldn't stay in the house anymore. So I left. I wandered the streets of Manhattan, and it was *cold*. It was cold even though it *wasn't* cold—it was summer.

I swear God was like, *This is the world without me.* I felt like I was walking around Gotham in a Batman movie—the faces in the shadows, the shadows themselves, the evil look in the eyes of men I passed on the sidewalks, huddled in corners. I'm convinced those artists' visions in comic books and in movies are a reflection of the world God showed me that night. A parallel world to our own that coexists here on Earth. The Devil's playground.

It was terrifying.

I called a friend who was also a believer to help me. She didn't know what to think about what I was saying. "Are you okay?" she asked.

I wasn't.

I didn't know if I was having a nervous breakdown or what, but at the same time I felt God had his hands on me. He kept telling me, *You are seeing exactly what the world is without me.*

My friend met me on the street, and we walked all the way up the West Side of Manhattan 'til we found a hotel called— coincidentally or not—the Inn.

I was like, *God, what are you telling me?*

We walked in, and they told us they had one room left.

A room at the Inn.

We took the room and stayed up all night, waiting for the coldness to pass. We prayed and thanked God together, and the next morning, I went back to my apartment. It was as if nothing had happened. It didn't feel scary anymore.

That's when all my emotions came pouring out.

In pure exhaustion I curled up on the floor in my bathroom and prayed: "God, I don't want to see that ever again. If seeing it was a gift, I don't *want* that gift. I'll do what I'm called to do."

I meant it. My faith was *good.* I believed. I never needed to see or feel the Devil's world—the world without the covering of Christ—again.

If I had only understood that the pain I felt was a *positive* thing, then maybe I wouldn't have taken all the blows so hard. The breakups, the heartbreak, the trouble I went through—it was God pushing people and situations out of my life that didn't serve my dream. If I had known, I could have embraced it. But as a result of going through that experience, I'm able to tell you to not hold on so tightly. To go ahead and shed. The pain of letting go is a *good* pain. Find comfort in knowing that the pain of shedding what doesn't serve your dream is part of the process of becoming the true you.

We're all here for a purpose, and mine is to inspire others to identify their passion and live their dream. Part of living that life is simply making choices to listen to the inspiration that's already inside you. Just by listening to that, by paying attention to and acting on your dream, you're going to get somewhere better.

Let me say that again: You're going to get somewhere *better*! Because our dreams are our road maps. *That's* the formula. *That's* the process that God gave us.

All you have to do is dance your dance, the unique dance that God gave *you*.

Even if you don't align with a particular church or religion, I still think it's fair to ask yourself whether your decisions are in alignment both with your dream and with something bigger than yourself and bigger than your worldly desires. When I chose not to strip, or when I saw a bowl of cocaine on the set of a music video but did not want to snort it—why did I make those choices? Those things happened before I aligned myself with any

The pain of letting go is a *good* pain. Find comfort in knowing that the pain of shedding what *doesn't* serve your dream is part of the process of *becoming* the true you.

particular religion. So why did I make what I firmly believe were the right decisions for me?

Because God lived in my dream.

I *believed* in my dream. I *trusted* my dream. I *held on to* my dream. That was my faith! That was *God*. And eventually God fully revealed himself to me because I was following him through my dream, and he wanted me to know him personally.

This is my truth. But you don't have to take my word for it. Just follow your dream, live your truth, and you'll find your own road to understanding.

The Big Truth

Dancing your truth is truly what matters. It will drive you. It will carry you. And when you trust it, it will become the process that will turn you into the superstar you are.

I've mentioned this already, but I want to say it again: the artists who move us and change the world almost never repeat what's already been done. They're the artists who dig down to their truths, who stand by what God gave them and deliver it despite all odds, despite all Dreamkillers. We know them when we see them, because we feel their gifts resonate when they dance or open their mouths to sing or spit their stories into a microphone.

Sometimes they touch their gifts so deeply that it resonates around the world.

Biggie Smalls—the Notorious B.I.G.—was one of those people.

He was such a great artist. He was Jamaican, like me, which made him my comrade and my soldier. And he was prolific.

He was an anomaly, a prototype. A storyteller, a poet, a world changer. A true original. And I was fortunate enough to get a chance to work with him because our particular gifts aligned at the perfect time.

Remember when I pitched Puff Daddy on a vision I had for a dance for Mary J. Blige? I'd imagined an elaborate dance that would dig back into the history of black music—to the 1920s and 1940s, to the Nicholas Brothers and the next-level tap mastery of Gregory Hines, to the old street culture of gangsters in double-breasted suits—but made modern, and strung together like a ballet.

Guess what? Puffy remembered it too.

It was 1996, and Biggie was set to make his performance debut at the Soul Train Awards in March. It was the first time he'd be featured on a big nationally televised awards show. He was a gangsta rapper, straight from the streets of Brooklyn; a kid who'd sold crack on the street corner before he made it in the music business; a man who'd turned his life around and now had a kid of his own with his wife, another artist named Faith Evans.

Puff knew it was a moment of significance for this groundbreaking gangsta rap master to be featured on national television in front of a wide audience. He knew Biggie needed to make an impression not just musically but visually.

It was time for hip-hop to elevate itself—and Puff called on *me* to put it together.

My vision for this "gangsta ballet," which had been evolving for a few years now, took on new meaning when I pictured Biggie at the center of it. There was something about Biggie that felt mysterious and unapologetic and otherworldly, so I focused on him as the Notorious B.I.G.: the Svengali, the savant, the orchestrator of the ballet.

The idea of men in zoot suits fell by the wayside. Instead, the dancers would all be women. And Biggie? He'd be in a full-on tuxedo, with top hat and tails. The girls would be in tux-like dance outfits, too, with top hats, tails, and character shoes. That's right—*heels*. No more combat boots and sneakers. Uh-uh. We were comin' at you straight outta Broadway.

I remember when I gave our hip-hop dancers their three-inch character shoes. They're like something you'd see in the musical *Chicago* or something the Rockettes might wear, and these girls from the hood were like, "Guurl, are you crazy?"

"Girls," I said, "just trust me. They're character shoes. It's theater. It's the razzle-dazzle."

If it weren't for Big and Puff trusting me with this, I think those girls might have walked out!

To the ghetto-fabulous look of the streets I added a top-hat look and a structure and organization that was charted like music, but these were notes that had never been played. This was hip-hop's moment to rise, the way jazz elevated from the speakeasies and clubs to the Broadway stage and the concert halls way back in the day. In my mind, Puffy and Biggie were like hip-hop's answers to Cab Calloway and Duke Ellington—prophets with the gifts to bring this art form out and up, from the streets to the masses.

For some reason, from the moment we met, Biggie trusted me and my vision. I'd tell him, "Big, you have this amount of time to get in place at the top of the stage with the dancers and your cane." Because he wasn't trained in the counts of dance or even the number of bars in music, I used his lyrics as the timing points to walk him through what he needed to do. "You have to get to the front of the stage by 'I stayed Gucci down to the socks,' and then do this by the 'Versace shades,' so the dancers can move around you. Can you make that happen for me?"

He was an artist within an artist. He was a thespian. He was a perfectionist. He rehearsed it, and he nailed it. No problem.

And Puff just *got* it. In fact, he got it so much that at the last minute he decided to insert himself right into the production: in a white tuxedo, complete with a top hat, seated at a big white grand piano (like Cab Calloway himself) at the start of the song. It was perfect. I slid it right into my overall idea.

The opening had Faith Evans at the top of this elaborate, modernized art deco set, as the dancers came out all around her. The spotlight hit Puffy, who was behind the piano, doing shout-outs to the audience to get everybody fired up. Then the Notorious B.I.G. descended in an art deco elevator, like a cage. The elevator doors opened up, and out he walked—a tortured bird freed!

There were so many layers to that performance, that vision I had, which I don't think anybody understood when I did it. Looking back now, I can see that there were layers that *I* didn't even understand. God knew more than any of us.

You can find that performance on YouTube. It was exactly the hip-hop ballet I envisioned, which Puffy was finally allowing me to produce because he wasn't nervous about keeping the street credibility anymore. He wanted performance, he wanted drama, he wanted *theater*—and that's exactly what he got.

That's exactly what America got.

That night, Biggie not only performed but won for Best R&B/ Rap Song of the Year. Rival rapper Tupac Shakur was backstage at the same time, and the producers had to separate their entourages because the tensions between Bad Boy Records (from NYC) and Death Row Records (from LA) had turned into a feud on a level I just didn't understand. I was just the little choreographer from Canada. I didn't know all these things were happening.

I carried some of the spirit of that piece over to the American Music Awards the following January, when I choreographed "If I Ruled the World" for Nas with Lauryn Hill. It was a more-modernized historical version of the gangster idea, based more on *The Godfather* than on something out of the golden age of musicals.

Two months later, on the night of the 1997 Soul Train Awards, after Biggie presented the R&B/Rap Song of the Year award to Toni Braxton, I met up with him at an after-party on Wilshire Boulevard.

I sat on his knee, and he hugged me and he said, "You saw that Nas copied us, eh, L? He copied our Soul Train performance." I didn't have the heart to tell him that I was the one who choreographed both performances. They weren't the same, and I don't think anyone else would have drawn the connection, but this was the beginning of my finding my true voice as a choreographer and artistic director—and the fact that Biggie recognized it, the fact that he caught the whole vibe of what I created and saw the connection to our work together, is just more proof of what an artist and visionary he was himself.

I swear Biggie was in a different place as a human being that night. He had come so far in the past year. He had been in a car accident, and he was walking with a cane. He talked about Faith Evans and their daughter—and about *faith*. It was like he'd made peace with God. He even wore a brand-new tattoo on his arm inspired by Psalm 27:

The Lord is my light and my salvation, whom shall I fear?

The Lord is the truth of my life, of whom shall I be afraid?

When the wicked, even my enemies and foes, came upon me

to bite my flesh, they stumbled and fell.

He was all of twenty-four years old, but he was already on a more beautiful path after coming so far and touching so many people with his truth. It was so good to see him. And I expected to see him again later that night, when the whole Bad Boy Records crew was set to meet up at the house we were all staying at in the Hollywood Hills. Some of us had gathered there earlier that day to watch the video for Biggie's new single, "Hypnotize," from his soon-to-be-released album.

I left the party with some of the crew and hopped in the car with my friend Kim Porter, Puffy's baby mama. We waved goodbye to everybody and went to the house.

But Biggie never got there.

The night I sat on his knee was the last night of his life.

He was gunned down in a drive-by shooting, just as Tupac had been gunned down six months earlier. Two great artists, murdered in cold blood, in two killings that remain unsolved to this day.

It was chaotic, but from what we understood, Puffy was *there*, in the very next car. He saw it all go down, and he was devastated. He was so upset that I couldn't even speak to him, because he was in such a medicated state.

The rest of the girls piled back in the car to head to the hospital to support Faith, but I stayed back. I didn't want any part of this. I called my mom, and even though it was the middle of the night in Jamaica, she picked up the phone.

"I don't know what to do, Mom. Big's dead. He's dead!"

"Get on a plane, child," she said. "Go home."

So that's what I did. I caught a ride to the airport and got on the next plane to New York City.

I was in that world, but I was not a part of that lifestyle. I had connected with Biggie as an artist, and we'd had a *moment* together, a moment that inspires me to this day. But I needed to go.

I still don't understand the seedy underside that exists in the hip-hop and rock-and-roll worlds. I don't want to. It's too close to what God showed me in New York, in the cold, parallel world of the Devil.

These artists seemingly want to become a better version of themselves and rise from their circumstances. But some are just too tempted to the instant gratifications of the other side. And some of them keep on rapping about it.

Art does imitate life. But I think there comes a time where you have to understand and be proud of your art and let it pull you up out of your circumstances.

I think most people who walked that fine line, who still lived the gangsta life even though they'd ascended to fame, realized that I wasn't about the street life. So they protected me. They honored and reverenced the God in me and the *gift* in me. What I learned up close is that a real gangster understands when the presence of the anointing is on somebody. They are closer to God than you might believe if you didn't know them. They understand that the Devil exists. They've seen him up close. So when they see someone living in their purpose, they understand they're seeing the evolution of someone becoming.

Why does that gangsta life still exist in entertainment? I'll never know for sure. But I think it's because it's the extension of another form of oppression. Because of the prejudice in the world, the oppression of a culture and a people, street life persists—and it gets sensationalized and glamorized. If we continue to create this image of a culture, and tell people what they're supposed to be and what they can't be and what they don't have access to, then that's what the next generation winds up aspiring to. So you can't judge someone who's in these circumstances. Instead, if you want to break the cycle, you have to create another option. That's what I believe God wants us to do: create the option.

If you feel pressured to connect to the street life we're talking about, I want you to know something: That is not your end. That is not your truth. That is something that might serve you in the short term, but if you continue to reach for your dream, you can come up out of it. It doesn't have to define you. It doesn't make you, and it definitely won't break you.

We need to give kids more access to this kind of inspiration. So much of what they have access to now says there's no hope: "You ain't gonna be nothin'. Stay in the hood. Stay in the ghetto. All you want is money. Selling weed, working the corner, that'll give you that money!"

No! There's a whole other option: following your dream.

It's me seeing myself in Alvin Ailey versus seeing a version of the typical black girl that the media has curated for me. It's me not allowing a white ballet teacher to tell me my feet are flat and my back is arched because I'm black, so I can't become the best version of myself as a prima ballerina. It's me defying that, denying that, not allowing that seed to take root because it's ignorant.

But that takes patience. It takes support. It takes at least some tiny bit of stability, like the stability my mom offered, which in many cases doesn't exist right now—especially from our government and our institutions. (Maybe that's a topic for another book.)

But the truth is that you can be who you are, who your dream calls you to be. It's been done! How many amazing stories are there of rappers and producers and actors and musicians and artists who rose up out of the projects and made lives for themselves? There are too many to count.

Be inspired by them. Be inspired by their stories.

And know that the only thing you *can't* be is the thing that came before.

You can't be the next Biggie Smalls, because that's already been done. He was the original. The prototype. One of *one.*

Be *your* original. *Your* prototype. *Your* one of one. That's how you'll succeed. That's how you'll become who you're meant to be.

I tell my artists all the time, "We're crayons in a box. Are you the same color as me? No. Do you *want* to be the same? We're *all* Crayola. We're *all* amazing. But when they call for the blue crayon, Ms. Yellow, can you *not* try to color like me? They asked for blue! Why are you scrubbing the page and trying to create blue when you're yellow?"

You don't want to be an imitation of anyone, because that's not what God meant for you.

Remember that you do not need to be the star or the famous one in order to be successful. Expressing your gift *is* the gift. The circumstances and the worldly spotlight are not the goal; the goal is to be the most authentically, expressively, artistically, creatively *you* that you can be. *That* is the way to rise to the capacity that God gives you.

Creativity can be found in the way you fold your towel, you

Be *your* original.
Your prototype.
Your one of one.
That's how you'll
succeed. That's how
you'll become who
you're meant to be.

know? The idiosyncrasies you have, the car you like, the color you want to buy—buy it! Don't get the same color as everybody else just so you fit in. That's how our creativity suffocates.

Let your creativity *breathe*.

The things you love that you lose yourself in, the things that make you happy and bring you joy—you're supposed to listen to that. It's *important* to listen to that. Don't tamp it down or be cynical about it. If you love taking long walks while listening to music, then put your favorite playlist into the Beats and go walk, because that is something you *need*. It's your spirit, your imagination, calling out to you and asking you for a requirement that will create a different flow in what you do every day. If you don't feed that part of you, it can't grow.

At any age, at any point in life, you can start paying attention to what you love and what you feel. But people sometimes have a problem paying attention to it because they've gone so long without addressing it that they've become a different version of themselves. So start right now!

We all need to take care of our physical health and our mental health—and too often we forget our *spiritual* health. I'm not talking about religion here; I'm saying that honoring your spirit is as simple as honoring those things that make you happy, those things that are joyful, those things in your childhood you did without thinking, without judging yourself, without fear. Those things are the beginning of you understanding the unique qualities that make you *you*. And because they were childlike, they were pure. You have to get back in touch with that. If you can find the bread crumbs that lead you back to the simple things that made you happy, that's a start.

Sometimes I go to Baskin-Robbins to get an ice cream cone,

because life seems too complex or I'm overthinking everything. I get to a point where I just need a Jamoca Almond Fudge on a sugar cone. Just that simple act realigns me with the feeling, the joy, the trust I have in myself. That taste on my tongue gives me perspective.

When you're forgetting to be creative, forgetting to do those things that make you happy, simply *not* doing what you usually do for everybody else will empower you; it will remind you to get back to a place where you're living the life you are meant to live.

Why is it that people judge themselves by what other people are doing? It is such a common problem. Why are they doing *that* instead of being present and dancing their own dance, and creating their own ballet, and creating their own rock-star community, and having their own fans? Like, be fans of your best friend. Be fans of your kids. Be fans of your spouse. Really. It's totally fine. Your *wife* can be your Beyoncé! Just that kind of give-and-take can help unlock the creativity in people that is so neglected, put aside, and not given a priority in life—both in you *and* in them!

As human beings we need to express our true selves in a creative way—even if it's working creatively on car engines or welding jobs. It does not matter what you do; it just matters that it's *yours*.

For me, expressing my truth was quickly evolving into a career of unlocking, unleashing, and building superstars who would get to live out and evolve *their* dreams.

STEP 6

Find Your Team

No one gets anywhere without a team.

Partnerships, contributors, the people who clear the way ahead of you—they all matter. If you find yourself feeling successful and you attribute it all to yourself, you're in for a wake-up call. It may not hit you today, but it *will* hit you—and hit you hard—when you let your team go or they just plain walk away, and you fall and can't get back up again, and you can't figure out why.

It's important to not only recognize those who help you along the way—including, of course, God—but also seek out people who align with your vision. People who will actually help you pursue and live your dream, not hurt you.

Unfortunately, even your friends can be enemies to your success if you're not careful. (Remember the "friend" who took me to the China Club?)

Honestly, I didn't have a lot of strong team members on my way up. I didn't have a lot of frontline encouragement from those with the vision to see me as something bigger than I was at any particular moment in time. Instead, I had more people who told me what I was missing, or why I wasn't right, or why I couldn't make it for one reason or another, than I had the kind of mentors and teachers who championed my gifts. But I now believe God wanted me to encounter those Dreamkillers so I would learn not to allow other people to plant seeds that would discourage or deny the existence of greatness in me, and so I would learn to encourage others to believe in *their* gifts rather than saying something that might stop them in their tracks.

It's important to not only *recognize* those who help you along the way—including, of course, God—but also seek out people who *align* with your vision. People who will actually *help* you pursue and live your dream, not hurt you.

The fact that I lacked the kind of mentors and teachers I wanted only sharpened my gift to become a strong mentor and teacher to others—including *you*. It sharpened my ability to lift up my students and artists and to teach them how to seek out and recognize the people in their lives who are truly on their side.

One person who definitely valued my talents was Puff Daddy, who had renamed himself P. Diddy back in 2001 but who always remained "Puffy" or "Sean" to me. He had seen my success in the industry to that point, and in 2005, he asked me to take my first frontline role on a reality television show, MTV's *Making the Band*. As their choreographer and artist-development mentor and coach, I was given the task of building a newly formed girl group from the ground up. I went to auditions all across America and chose five women (out of thousands) who would ultimately become the bestselling girl group Danity Kane.

By the time I joined the series, I was not only a highly sought-after choreographer but the person the industry turned to when it came to breaking new ground with new artists. I had already worked in that capacity for Lil' Kim, Mary J. Blige, Brandy, JoJo, Whitney Houston, and many more. But my work was behind the scenes. This time, my work would happen in front of a camera, where millions of viewers would see me, learn my name, and see my personality in action. But the version they saw left out a big part of who I am.

Reality TV was still kind of new in those days. It was the Wild West of television, and people were just figuring it out as they went along. What I didn't realize was that on most reality shows the editors were using the footage they had to create "characters" in the editing room. TV calls for drama, and somehow, by cutting different scenes and situations from different angles, and putting reactions from one moment into another moment, the *Making the Band* editors managed to show a much angrier, less inspirational version of me than what I was in real life. On my second season, when I worked with the boy band Day26, the producers and editors and even Diddy himself made me out to be a full-on villain.

To be fair, I lost my cool more than once during filming. Things were crazy. I was commissioned by Puff Daddy to build a supergroup from nothing. We were practicing and working and filming practically round the clock, with no breaks, for a tiny paycheck. The stakes were high as could be because Puff's expectation of my work was so high.

I was also still young and in the process of learning how to collaborate with a team that didn't always see my vision or respect my perspective. I was still in the process of becoming the coach and mentor and visionary I would someday be.

Learning to be a team player is just as important as finding your team. It was a big struggle at first, because I was *very* passionate. Obviously, when you're coaching people into greatness and pulling out of them the confidence to be fearless, you *want* your coach to be as dedicated to the vision as possible. When the going gets tough, you need someone who believes in the vision, sometimes even more than *you* do, to pull you across those hard days. I honestly think that's one of my strongest gifts, but the editors didn't treat it like it was a gift. They edited my passion down into something angry, feisty, even outrageous at times.

I think it was also surprising for some people to see what happened behind the scenes and what it really takes to make it to the top. They had no idea what the real process looked like, and they were seeing it for the very first time. Anything that breaks new ground requires the very best of you—and that isn't always pretty to look at on camera.

As we filmed, the producers on the show would throw the girls in the studio with me just to see what happened. Remember: I *love* the process, because the greatness is in the process. Because I was so high on the creative energy, it was like giving a painter every single paintbrush and every color known to mankind, and letting her go.

I tried everything with them—things like working with hats, canes, chairs—while also exploring the crucial aspects of artist development, such as how you walk, talk, sit, and present yourself onstage and on camera. They were young girls who wanted to feel that they were on their road to success, so they ate it up. If I had a hard day, which happens, they would go back to the house and complain about me. That wouldn't be a big deal in real life. But when you capture it on film, and you take me yelling and screaming for ten seconds here and there and edit it as if I did all that yelling and screaming at one time, it looks ugly.

There were times when I would verbally push one of the girls and say something like, "You know better, because you're *great*!" and the editors would leave off the "because you're great." They'd show me yelling, "You know better!" which just made me sound mean.

The thing is, my true character never changed. Sometimes I post clips online from the old *Making the Band* in which I'm saying something positive to my artists, and people ask if it's from a new series: "Did you just shoot that?"

I'm like, "No. That's from the first era."

And they come back with "Oh. I don't remember you being so nice on that show!"

Those clips are clear evidence of me choosing my truth. The real me *did* shine through, even then. Not even the best editors could change my intention for greatness. They couldn't change the core of who I am, because *I* didn't change it.

The results of the work we did were undeniable: Danity Kane went from being a bunch of girls who didn't know one another to having the number-one album in the country.

The process works. The dedication works. The artistry *works*!

The same kind of measurable success happened the next season, when I helped put the boy band Day26 on the R&B charts. But as that unfolded, I was unaware of the chatter that was going on above me and around me. There were people on Puffy's team who thought I was getting too big for my own good—maybe taking too much credit, getting too popular with the audience—and they wanted to put a stop to that.

If I was popular with the audience, I didn't know it. We didn't have social media feeding our likes and dislikes on a minute-to-minute basis back then. And my head wasn't big about what I'd accomplished. I was just proud of what the *groups* had accomplished by working so hard, and by going through the process of becoming groups together.

I think some of the people around Puffy at the time were also intimidated or bothered by the connection that Puff and I had. It was never, ever anything romantic. Never. But we'd known each other for ten years or so by that point, and there was obviously a serious artist-to-artist, destiny-to-destiny, purpose-driven connection between us. I loved him like family. I still do! He's such a genius, and from the beginning, he was always who he was. He was always very much a king in his kingdom, and he was the established leader, and he had a strength that was inspiring to me.

Not everyone could have done what he did; it's incredible. But not everyone could have done what *I* did, standing next to and collaborating with that type of individual over a long period of time.

At any rate, just as jealousy bit me on my first big break with *Malcolm X*, it came back around to bite me on *Making the Band*.

The footage is out there for the whole world to see. One day, after all of these people got in Diddy's ear, Diddy walked into the room and confronted me with cameras rolling. He accused me of being bold and braggadocious, and I shot back: "No, not for *me*. For the artist! I'm fighting for my *artist*!"—which was the absolute truth. "That's what I'm *supposed* to do."

Suddenly he and his entourage started attacking me, personally, in ways I'd never been spoken to before, using language no one had ever used toward me in my entire life.

So I walked out.

I was so scared by the intimidation, on and off camera, that I went straight to the police station and filed a report. I felt I had to protect myself.

People in the industry said, "Why are you doing this? You know Puffy's going to blackball you. You won't be able to get another job!"

But I was like, "Did you not hear the way he spoke to me? Did you not hear the way they all tried to come at me? That's not right. I'm just a young woman. I don't deserve that."

I turned to God, and he gave me a window of escape. I would never think of Diddy as less than family, but sometimes family and friendship get tested. And true greatness, true respect, survives the battle.

The beautiful thing now, all these years later, is that Puff and I are closer than ever. We're family—and we're rebooting *Making the Band*! We celebrated his fiftieth birthday party together. He's one of my best friends. And on the night before the 2020 Grammys, at the Clive Davis party, which is the hottest party in town, Diddy got up and spoke about how I inspired *him*. (I'll share more about this in the last chapter.) And I think there was a lesson there: it was his people, his team, who got between us. It's so important to have the *right* people around you at all times.

At the time, though, how I left the show was traumatizing. I felt misunderstood, and this fabricated image of me spilled over and affected my real life. Because of the character people saw on *Making the Band*, my phone stopped ringing. People saw what they believed was someone angry, someone they didn't want their artists to be around. It would take me a while to fight back into the business and get choreography gigs again after that.

A lot of people just didn't trust me. They saw the "reality" program and assumed that it was real! So when I went in for a choreography gig, managers and handlers would be like, "Well, you know, we're going to have to sit in on the meeting. We just want to make sure they're comfortable in the room with you." I had to endure that for a couple of *years*.

Many people don't understand the self-sacrifice that so many artists and creative people have to go through in order to achieve the goal and the dream. Getting to greatness, or getting to others' greatness, takes more than just being nice or being liked.

Greatness is not achieved by having a coach who tells you, "You did great today!" when your voice is fried and you're not hitting a note.

There are too many of those people in the world. I call them *Yessigans*, because they're like hooligans who will yes you to death.

A Yessigan is a person who will deny you access to the truth. If an artist says, "I want to set my clothes on fire because I think that'd be great for the performance," the Yessigan says, "Yes, that sounds like a great idea"—which causes the artist to wind up in the hospital with burns all over his body.

Yessigans like to keep people on a hamster wheel where they make money off what *they* can control, what *they* know. They're leeches, and they disguise themselves as loyal assistants, staffers, managers and bosses, even family members. They stagnate your growth and creativity—because growth and creativity aren't something the Yessigans really care about.

Unfortunately, a lot of people in the entertainment industry (and other industries too) are loyal to the check rather than the choice. And when you're loyal to the check, that ends. The dollars that come in are just a number. They can't produce anything new. Even when something is successful, reproducing what's already been done has a shelf life.

On the other hand, if you're loyal to the choice, if you align with the growth and creativity that got you there in the first place, you can always have rivers of running water overflow, you know? You'll be willing to take the risks, and follow your dreams, because you know it's the creativity within you that led to whatever monetary success you have in the first place. When you're loyal to the choice to live by your dream, then you're already growing into what's next. *Then* the check will come. The abundance will come!

In order to sustain and grow into the fullness of your dream, rooting out the Yessigans and surrounding yourself with people who help you make the right choices for you and your artistry is a must.

When you're *loyal* to the choice to live by your dream, then you're already *growing* into what's next.

Whenever I'm challenged by professional doubters, I let them know I have no time for smallness. Greatness is fulfilled, not bought or manipulated. It requires a process and a period of faith. Do you have enough faith to allow greatness to be fulfilled? Or are you gonna doubt and try to limit your success to the box you're in right now?

When you take that first step toward trusting your voice, there's what I call a moment of suspension, when you're out there by yourself. It feels like you're walking on the moon. But then the rhythm changes and you get back into what you have created— this new space, this new art, this new place, this new level, this new freedom in yourself, this new muscle, this new *thing*. You reach a spot where even the doubters can't deny that something's happening, when you're in rhythm with who you really are and it feels *different*. It happens to everyone who sticks it out through the doubt.

It's funny: once I fight through the doubters and get the vision to where it's supposed to be, they all get happy.

There are lots of professional doubters in the world, and every artist or creative person will be surrounded by them both before and after success comes along. My advice is this: Go right through them. Go around them. Stay on your toes, like a boxer, and block, block, block if you have to. Keep them in their place. And if you don't have the strength to block them all yourself, make sure you have people around you (like me!) to do the blocking for you.

Despite the closed doors and resistance I went through after *Making the Band*, despite feeling like I'd lost my team by losing my connection to Puffy and the artists he worked with, I chose to keep going. No matter what. No matter how hopeless I felt in the moment.

The pathway God made clear to me wasn't just a continuation of where I was; it was a pathway that would carry me to heights I'd been aiming for ever since I was a little girl.

Going Gaga

I first met Lady Gaga in a dirty studio, in a bad part of town, at a point in her career when almost nobody knew her name. She had been through a few managers and tried wearing different hats, leaving her birth name of Stefani Germanotta behind along the way. She had been dropped by two different record labels and had no idea where to go next.

When we found each other, we were both broken birds. The girl I met that day showed no evidence—*none*—of the superstar she would become.

And I had no idea that I was walking into the opportunity that would place me where I always dreamed of being. Someone else might have looked at Gaga in that moment and thought, *Nuh-uh. I'm not dedicating my time and talents to someone who's starting from so far down.* This girl couldn't look at herself in the mirror. She'd been rejected and was feeling dejected in just about every way.

She handed me a cassette that we put in a boom box, and we listened to a song she'd written. I started to move. She mimicked my movements a little bit, and I saw something that only the gift within me could see: a diamond in the rough.

The song was "Paparazzi."

I asked her what her interpretation of the song was, and she told me, "I feel it's about the parties, the cocaine, the highs . . ."

I said, "No. It's a love song about your dream. The paparazzi, the fame . . ." I interpreted it based partly on my own biography and the stories of the artists I'd seen rise and fall around me. I began to build a vision of her biggest appetite, the fame itself— and the idea that often, when you love fame so much, it takes over and consumes you.

Fame is what Lady Gaga wanted, and so far the record industry had told her that everything she had to offer was a failure. They rejected her songs, her look, her style, and she truly did not know what else to do.

She was an open book, a blank slate, looking for guidance, looking for just one person to believe in her.

That one person was me.

I decided to pour everything I had into Gaga, into unlocking *her* dream, into unleashing *her* creativity, to see just how far God would allow my gift to go. Could I take an artist who'd been broken down to absolutely nothing and build her into a superstar?

This girl was clearly a dreamer. But it was more than that. Almost immediately, she responded to my vision. She showed up. She was willing to put in the work. If I told her to lift her left hand, she lifted her left hand. If I told her to take a step, she took a step.

When she started to see results, she responded with more energy. She told me she couldn't dance, so I watched the way she tapped her foot and the way she seemed to feel the music when she sang. She always put the stress on the offbeats, the one and the three. So I asked her to move with me—one shoulder up, one shoulder down—on the offbeats, which isn't the way dancers typically dance. The more we did it, the more I was able to unleash her unique style.

She was driven. She kept practicing. Long hours, long days, long nights. She could hardly believe what was happening. By following my direction, she started *dancing*. She watched herself in the mirror, and she liked what she saw.

We carried this creative energy into everything. I helped develop a whole world for her—a vision of odd and offbeat looks that would carry into her videos, her live shows, her whole being. How she moved, how she sat, how she spoke, how she conducted herself on camera and off: a culmination of all the artist-development growth I'd explored and perfected in all my years in the business.

During our first few weeks together, I envisioned the beginnings of what would become the Monster Ball—the groundbreaking world tour that was still years in the future. I had dreamed of something as grand and strange and groundbreakingly spectacular as the Monster Ball Tour from the time I was twelve years old. I thought, *If this broken bird keeps working this hard, she could very well bring this vision to life.*

From two completely different backgrounds, two completely different worlds, two completely different paths, God led us to this intersection at the very same time. The lessons I had to share, the gifts I had to give, and the vision I had to offer were exactly what Lady Gaga needed at that moment, and Lady Gaga was the blank slate I needed to finally understand the fullness of my gifts, my abilities, and my dream.

How is that even possible? Only God knows.

Because I recognized God's gift in me, God's greatness in me, God's dream in me, which was bigger than any person (including myself) could understand, I saw how to pull greatness from *her*—the God-given greatness of a world-changing entertainer. And that's exactly what I'm attempting to do for *you*!

No matter where you are in your life or career, you can still become who you're meant to become. No matter how much rejection you've faced, or how far you think you've fallen, you can stand up and rise. If you have the capacity to conquer the world, to reach the top, you can! But no matter what your capacity might be—which only God truly knows—you can reach down deep, get in touch with your dream, and reignite the fire in your heart and spirit, right now. And you can do so even if you think no one else supports that dream you have—because *I* do. I'm on your team. I believe in you.

At some point down the road, after Gaga hit number one on the charts and was getting all kinds of praise for her looks and her confidence and her dancing in her videos and live shows— the fulfillment of growing into the vision I had for her from day one—she told me that she once had a dance teacher who told her she couldn't dance.

When Gaga told me that she couldn't dance, that wasn't her speaking; she was just repeating what she'd been told, what she'd been falsely led to believe by one Dreamkiller way back when she was young and impressionable. It was astounding to me: she had her own Mr. Christopher in her life! And the power that one person exerted over her with his words had nearly kept her from everything that Lady Gaga would eventually become, everything she had ever dreamed for herself.

She should never have believed that dance teacher. That seems obvious now, right? And *you* should never have believed whoever told you that you couldn't or shouldn't do whatever your dream was, whether it was back in your young and impressionable days or even yesterday. Let that negativity go! Drop it! Get rid of it!

That person was not on your team, was not on your side, and was not supporting the gift that God clearly gave to you. Let this story be the lesson that encourages you that you absolutely *can* and *should* dance your dance in life, in any way you want to, like no one has ever danced before you.

Work to find the people, or even the *one person*, who will see you as the diamond in the rough the way I saw Gaga. Use this book to unleash the passion in you so you can live your dream the way Gaga was able to realize her dream through me.

Once Lady Gaga saw that my inspiration, vision, and experience were working for her, there was no looking back. The same should be true for you: trust your dream, trust your passion, and you'll get to where God truly wants you to go.

Before you read this book, you might have expected success to come to you in a certain package, looking a certain way. Clearly, it doesn't. Sometimes, as it was for me, success comes to you at your lowest point. It comes in a dirty studio, as a broken-down bird; a piece of coal that's ready to face the fire and the pressure, to be cut and polished into the diamond that exists within.

Gaga was fearless about doing the work it took to unlock all of that. I want you to know that you can be fearless too. After everything you've read, after witnessing the example of my life and work as proof that these steps work, I hope it's clear that you have nothing to fear at all.

Branching Out

Success begets success, and that's as true in the entertainment world as anywhere else. So while Lady Gaga was hitting number one, I wound up getting called to do all sorts of amazing things. Like working with Katy Perry to create the look and movement for her "California Gurls" video in 2009, which was *so* much fun. And guess who else called me? Puffy! He and *Survivor* and *The Apprentice* creator Mark Burnett had come up with a new show called *Starmaker*. Because they'd both witnessed the kind of massive star-making I'd been a part of lately, they asked me to share my expertise on their show. Puffy and I let bygones be bygones, and I said yes.

It was only the start.

In 2010, between working on Lady Gaga's videos for "Telephone" and "Alejandro" and choreographing her live performances on just about every music awards show there was, I said yes when I was asked to become a judge on the *Dancing with the Stars* spin-off *Skating with the Stars*. And then I said yes to offers for two different reality shows in which I would be featured front and center: *The Dance Scene* on E!, which followed my dance team and me through the grueling work of preparing for performances for a variety of artists; and *Born to Dance*, a new dance competition show that culminated in awarding a previously unknown dancer a $50,000 prize. Both of those shows debuted in 2011, eventually leading me to roles on *Dance Moms* and *So You Think You Can Dance*. All of these opportunities meant that I was now fulfilling my gift as a mentor, teacher, and coach in ways that were bigger than I'd ever dreamed. I was instilling passion and positivity in young dancers all around the world!

I was busier than I'd ever been, and I was fully engulfed in living my dream. It was a little ironic that I was finally getting publicly recognized for my role and influence in the dance world right at the time I was growing out of my position as purely a choreographer. I was much more excited about growing into the much bigger role of director, creative director, and visionary for Lady Gaga and other artists.

For her 2011 performance at the Grammy Awards of "Born This Way," the first single from Gaga's album of the same name, I couldn't shake this vision of her emerging from a vessel of sorts, an egg at the top of the stage—birthing herself into the world. (It was only *after* this performance that my mother reminded me about how I'd choreographed myself out of the box in the basement at age seven.)

Gaga loved it. I directed the costumes, the set design, the quirky shape of the stairs—because Gaga couldn't walk down any *ordinary* stairs in this world of lovable freaks and outcasts that had emerged through the Monster Ball Tour. I oversaw *everything* for both that Grammys performance and the tour itself—as I did for every show, television, and stage performance she did for seven or eight straight *years*—pushing our team of talented set designers and costume designers and lighting directors and more to join us in this vision to create what became one of the most memorable and talked-about performances in the history of the Grammys. Considering the performances that have rocked the world from that show, including unforgettable moments from Michael Jackson, Madonna, and more, that's saying something!

By the time the Monster Ball Tour was over, we were on top of the world. By almost any measure, Lady Gaga was the biggest pop star on the planet. My vision for her fame had been fulfilled.

My work was *done*.

I don't blame Gaga, or any other artist, for falling prey to some of the Yessigans around her once she hit that level. Worldwide fame brings a whole new invasion of doubt and insecurity, especially in artists who've struggled with those feelings their whole lives. When you get to what the world perceives as the top—and I believe this applies not only to people in entertainment but also CEOs in the business world and politicians who get elected and especially re-elected—it affects you. And you can't always keep the proper perspective all by yourself, because you're inside your head and your process, and you wind up overthinking things. That's why you need support from a solid team. We *all* do. At the very least we need a friend or a family member who can say, "Maybe you're overthinking this," or whatever you happen to need in your moment of self-doubt or self-obsession. You need a person or two or three who will stand up and have your back enough to say, "Hey, let's just take a step back and rethink a few things."

It is so important to be able to trust the people around you and know that they really do have your best interests at heart. To trust that they're not fighting only for themselves. That's where the Yessigans become most destructive: when they turn you against your true friends, the true collaborators, the ones who put your creative vision first.

If you ever find yourself in a position of power and success, I beg of you: talk to those who were with you in the beginning, who stayed true on your ride to the top, and ask them to give you a reality check. The reality check that a true believer and friend and team member is likely to offer has very little to do with *themselves* and everything to do with what serves your dream.

In *The Wizard of Oz*, Dorothy never would have defeated the Wicked Witch of the West without the help of the Lion, the Scarecrow, the Tin Man, and even a little wake-up nudge from Glenda, the Good Witch of the East. And they all needed to believe in one another in order to realize, when they pulled back the curtain, that Oz wasn't what he said he was.

Finding your people, your team, and sticking by them is important.

You'll never make it without them.

And as I said at the beginning of the chapter, to not honor your team, the contributors who had your back on the way up— well, that's just not cool.

I'm convinced that the falling-out between Lady Gaga and me—just as in the falling-out between Puffy and me—wasn't about the two of us at all. Instead, some of the people around her thought I shouldn't be working with other artists. I shouldn't be getting my own TV show. I shouldn't be taking offers to do other things that would further my own career and my own gift. They thought that I was taking too much spotlight—even though I didn't *want* her spotlight—and they would be better off without me.

Just as I realized this chatter was happening, Gaga fired me. In an *email*. I'm not even sure she wrote it herself. How can we be sure of anything when we don't look each other in the eye and communicate with our voices and our spirits?

If I had done something wrong, if my vision for her had failed, maybe it would have made more sense to me. But by this point in my career, I knew I couldn't fight the Yessigans in her life, not if those were the people she wanted to believe. She was dancing her dance. I was dancing mine. I knew I'd be okay.

I just hoped she'd be okay too.

STEP 7

Step into Purpose

After Lady Gaga fired me, I knew what I had to do. I had learned God's lessons well by then. I had to stay in my gift. I had to trust that this was the path God wanted for me. And despite feeling like I was falling, God helped me to remember the truth: what I was *really* doing was growing.

After all I'd accomplished, all the new heights I'd reached, I was more prepared than ever to step forward into whatever God wanted from me next.

One of the first people who contacted me after the news of my firing broke was Puff Daddy. He didn't call to offer condolences. He called with a new opportunity: He and James Cruz had started managing a new girl by the name of Nicki Minaj. She had a successful mixtape, but she wasn't a superstar. She had talent and a major pen. She wrote her own songs, and she had such a powerful presence—but she still needed *more* to break her through to a wider audience. They needed to create a vision for her, and they asked me if I could do it.

Was it a step down in some people's eyes? The naysayers, the critics, the moneymen who assumed my career was over because I wasn't sticking with the already established pop star? Sure, it was. A big one. To go from working with an artist with millions of fans to one who was just starting out was like the CEO of a billion-dollar company stepping down to run a start-up.

That's exactly why it was so exciting.

I didn't hesitate for one second, because I knew this was God calling.

I was never one to ride coattails or stick with the status quo. I was a visionary, a builder. That's my role. You can't be afraid that what you've built is the only thing you can build and, therefore, not continue to evolve. You can't trust your dream based on other people's opinions of it.

I had built plenty of acts at that point, and with Gaga I had started completely from scratch and worked as the creative director, the visionary, the choreographer, the designer, the *everything* to help turn her into the number-one pop star on the planet. That's where my dream had brought me. I'd *accomplished* that. My purpose was about the act of building, the vision of seeing what's not yet there. It was time for me to step into that part of my dream, to step into that purpose with another start-up artist, even if other people thought I was crazy to do so.

"I'll take it," I said.

Turns out, Nicki and I were aligned with another idea that went all the way back to our childhoods. She had this idea to turn herself into a new kind of Barbie for the black girls of the world, and I was *there for it*. I had been there since I was down under the stairs in my parents' basement in a Toronto suburb. So I built her a two-story Barbie house for her live shows and her first big TV appearances, and she launched her career in a way that earned her something like $45 million in the next couple of years.

What we created was more than just visuals and choreography and a look. It served as inspiration the likes of which neither of us ever expected. Her die-hard fans loved the whole thing so much they named themselves the Barbz. And the Barbz became a force to be reckoned with. Thanks to social media, they're a tight-knit bunch of millions of women all across the country, and there have been articles about how they stand strong together—not only in support of the music they love, but politically. The Barbz have been known to sway elections in the US. How crazy is that?

Almost overnight, I helped to build a whole new brand for Nicki. A brand that I love and cherish to this day. A brand that allowed her to live *her* dream!

This is the power of *my* dream in action.

By this point, I hope you realize that *you* are my artist—and my vision for you is to align yourself with your passion and live your dream. Take my advice and experience and use all of it for *you*.

Even if you don't think you're up to it right this second; even if you're feeling the failing, the falling, or the firing; even if everything isn't going your way and you feel like you're back to square one because you messed something up or something didn't go the way you hoped and planned, have faith. When you stay true to your dream, there is always something more that comes from it. Sometimes that something takes you exactly where you need to be.

Second Chances, Second Dances

When I was fired from *Malcolm X* by Otis Sallid, way back at the beginning of my career, I learned a hard lesson. After suffering the consequences of not living up to his expectations of me, I changed how I handled myself. In fact, since then I've been crazy about being on time. I never do anything the night before a gig that could mess with my ability to wake up in the morning. Forget about going to the club; I don't go shopping at *Target* the night before an important meeting. Even if someone I love asks me to hang out at night, I won't go. I won't let anything stand in the way of waking up fresh and arriving on time to wherever I'm expected.

But Otis Sallid didn't dismiss me entirely just because I messed up that one day. I stayed in his classes. I kept training with him. And when the movie was done filming and it was time to go into the studio for some Foley work and overdubs to get the sound just right, Otis recommended me to Spike Lee. He gave me a second chance to dance! Even though I had zero experience, the two of them brought me in for this intricate part of the filmmaking process, in which any sound issues are fixed and things like footsteps and dance steps are dubbed over so that what you see on the screen matches what you hear through the speakers.

It was fun! Matching the steps of the dancers on-screen while the mic on the floor under my feet picked up my sounds was a challenge, but I took right to it.

I also got along well with Spike Lee. We ran into each other from time to time in the years after that, and we both watched each other from afar as our careers progressed. Then one day in the early 2000s, when I was in the middle of doing choreography for Brandy's first big tour, Spike called me.

"I need you to do the choreography for this artist, for this video I'm shooting," he said. "But I can't tell you who it is."

It was a very Spike Lee thing to do.

"Okay, but like, *when*?"

"Now."

"I can't. I'm in LA, and I can't leave Brandy," I said.

"All right," he said. "Then I'll tell you: it's Michael Jackson."

I just about dropped the phone.

"Okaaay," I said. "Just a second."

I covered the phone with my hand. "Um, Brandy? Can I talk to you for a second?"

I told her what was up, and her jaw dropped. She was like, "No. Uh-uh. Just *go!*"

She wasn't even mad at me. It was *Michael Jackson!*

The video was for the song "They Don't Really Care About Us," and Spike already had the vision of it playing out like a jail scene. I hopped into that vision and got to work, the same way I got to work for any other artist. But this *wasn't* any other artist. First of all, it was Spike Lee, a visionary of film like no other. And second, it was Michael Jackson! The whole experience was just on another level.

The whole time I was there with him, with this icon, I was privileged to stand next to his gift. Not the man—the *gift*. And there was nothing like that gift. I'd show him a move and he'd do it with a flair that was even better than I'd imagined. Every movement was effective immediately because he understood the intention behind it. He just got it.

Understanding how to stay in your gift and retain its blessings even as you deal with the rest of your worldly life—I swear that could be a whole other book. But the best way to do it is to find your supporters—the ones who will have your back no matter what; the ones who recognize when you're in your gift and when you're out of it and will let you know the difference—and then listen to them.

And the best way to do *that* is to listen closely to what God is telling you and do everything you can to block out the voices of confusion that come from someplace else.

I have no doubt that Michael was directly in touch with his gift. I had the great privilege of working with him when he was in it, and he was *magnificent*. He had perfected surrendering to the gift of *becoming*, and onstage he completely lived what it means to say yes to the power of your truth.

Watching the video for "They Don't Really Care About Us" and thinking back to that moment will never get old for me.

Realizing how it came about makes it all the sweeter.

When God taught me the lesson about responsibility and living up to expectations, he was also trying to teach me that failing can be a good thing. A *great* thing—as long as you don't let go of your dream.

If I hadn't failed, there's a chance Otis might not have had me in mind when he thought about dancers for the Foley and overdub work on *Malcolm X*. If I hadn't failed, maybe I wouldn't have had the chance to connect with Spike Lee in a way that he would remember me. Maybe he wouldn't have thought of me a decade later when he needed a choreographer to work with Michael Jackson, and thought of me *again* when he needed a choreographer to work with him on a Pepsi commercial with Beyoncé. (I almost forgot to mention that one!)

I didn't see it at first. I didn't see it in my early twenties. But as I got older, I realized that when something ended or seemed disappointing in the immediate moment, what appeared to be a failed step or a misstep never was. Even as a choreographer, I've seen that a lot of my more brilliant ideas and new directions come after I miss a step. It's amazing; when you miss a step, your gift allows you to see what might come next. It's there, it's God-given, it's already a part of who you are. It's your *why*. It's just the artist's way: the sculptor who breaks a piece only to reveal a new vision for his work; the guitarist who hits a wrong note and suddenly envisions a new melody. When we're open to God's good work, mistakes and failures are almost never a bad thing. In fact, I've come so far now that even in the middle of getting bad news about a project or a canceled gig or a decision that's not going my way or a relationship that's on the rocks—even if the news is painful and awful to hear—I stop myself from getting upset about it.

Instead, I recognize the feeling and replace any worry or fear or pain with a feeling of thankfulness to God. And I speak it right out loud: "Thank you, Lord. This news is not what I expected, but I know that it is right for me. I know that this isn't a step backward—it's a step *forward* into your purpose for me." (Can I tell you how much easier life gets when you trust that God has your back? When you trust that your dream is yours, no matter what?)

What other people refer to as "missteps" and "failures" are just God course-correcting, deepening, perfecting your purpose, your capacity to become.

It's like when a dancer falls out of a pirouette but the next step is even better than anyone anticipated. That step—the one you've never seen before, the one that innovates the movement and takes it into the future—happened only because of the fallout. The recovery led to a step that was actually more original than anything the choreographer had planned on doing, and the choreographer recognized that and included it in the dance. Now it's the new standard.

When God is your choreographer, that happens all the time: when you fall out of something and you trust him, you become what you're supposed to be.

The falling out produces the greatness and allows you to step forward.

When you fall out of what you thought you were capable of *yesterday*, you step into *tomorrow*. And I swear that when you trust it, when you feel it, when you acknowledge and honor it, you will have a physical, spiritual reaction to what God is trying to pull out of you.

Disappointment and loss fall by the wayside once you recognize that the bumps and the blocks are necessary in order to perfect you in the process.

There is no "risk." There is no "failure." It's all just part of your process. To focus on worrying about risk and failure makes you a victim in a system that wants to keep you down. Reject it!

Failure is a worldly word. It's not the language of love, the language of dreams, the language of God.

My whole life has been full of trying, and failing, and therefore growing—of stepping into God's purpose, for *me*.

Can I tell you how much I failed at the beginning? It went far beyond my failing to fulfill my promise on the set of *Malcolm X*.

I followed Jennifer Lopez out to LA after she moved there to be a Fly Girl on *In Living Color*. I took a shot at dozens of auditions for shows and movies—and I didn't get a single gig. Why? Because I wasn't sexy enough, tall enough, pretty enough, white enough, black enough, *anything* enough in that town. New York City was all about the grit, the drive, the determination, the power, the hunger, the energy, the creativity. And Los Angeles was all about the surface, how you looked, how you fit, what you wore—or, more accurately, what you *didn't* wear. It was awful.

I had producers and directors tell me flat out that I should get a boob job and come back later; get butt injections and try again; get my teeth whitened, get my hair straightened, get a makeup artist, wear colored contacts, wear higher heels, show more skin—and that's not even counting the offers to hit the casting couch in exchange for a lousy job that wouldn't even pay my bills.

Disappointment and *loss* fall by the wayside once you recognize that the bumps and the blocks are *necessary* in order to perfect you in the process.

My femininity, my curves, my sexiness didn't kick in for a few years after that. Can you imagine if I'd started adding all kinds of silicone and fillers to my body when I was that young? There is no way I would be the sexy and confident woman I am today. I look at these little girls—the seventeen- and eighteen- and twenty-two-year-olds who come out for auditions and don't think their bodies are enough—and I tell them: "Give yourself a chance to grow into yourself so the inside *does* match the out-side. If you allow that process, if you love what God gave you, the fact that you have crooked teeth, or whatever you think is 'wrong' with you right now, is going to be the exact reason why someone wants you to be the lead in a movie. As you mature and understand that, you're not going to *want* to straighten your teeth. And if you *do*, later on, at least the decision will be yours and not be based on you not feeling attractive enough or talented enough."

If only we could see the end.

Only God can see the end. So trust him.

If someone is telling you the gap in your teeth is wrong, and you don't align with that feeling, don't change it. If you like the gap in your teeth, then stay aligned with *you*.

And remember: your "failings" are you stepping *forward*, if you just believe.

How I Got Back

I slept on J.Lo's couch in LA because I couldn't afford a hotel or an apartment out there. But I still needed to pay my rent back in New York City. I had bills to pay, and I couldn't pay 'em. I was so fed up by all the rejections that I got angry—so angry that I was essentially fearless when I finally went to an audition for a video for Sir Mix-a-Lot's "Baby Got Back."

I knew I didn't have any "back" to speak of. So I went in thinking, *I'm really gonna go to try out for a 'Baby Got Back' video and take this seriously? I'm an Alvin Ailey–trained dancer!* But I needed money. I needed to *sustain*.

Lucky for me, the failings and rejections made me smarter than my circumstances. I knew I wasn't gonna make it on my looks. I needed something else. Something more.

Okay, well, what do I need to do to feel this beat and get this check?

The audition was at Screenland, a huge, intimidating space where all the big auditions happened. My friend Roberto drove me there in his broken-down jalopy. I watched some of the big-busted, apple-bottomed girls with their teased-up hair going into the audition, and I knew I needed to get *creative* if I was gonna make it.

I could've changed into a leotard or a bikini—but the idea hit me before I got out of the car.

Boom-*kack*! I would walk in looking like *none* of those other girls.

I was always into James Dean, and I liked the whole 1950s tough-guy look. I noticed that Roberto was carrying a pack of Newports.

"Hey, give me those," I said. I put them in the sleeve of my T-shirt and rolled up the sleeves, just like James Dean did. Instead of changing into dance shoes, I kept my combat boots on, which I wore with shorts and fishnets. I tied the T-shirt just above my belly button and painted my lips bright red.

Coming up with that whole rebellious, sort of angry, sort of punk look in that moment—I swear, that was God's way of seeding the creative visionary I would later be for other artists.

How do I know? Because I got the gig!

When I danced, Sir Mix-a-Lot was like, "Whatever she's on, I want some of *that* in my video. She's a *star*."

I had on more clothes than anyone else did. It wasn't about showing skin. It was about the attitude, the gift, the talent, and the creativity it took to stand out in the crowd.

I was *done* with LA shutting me down. I was not going to continue to let their no be my yes. I was like, "Uh-uh. I gotta go with *my* yes every time."

I booked the job, and it was the highest-paying video I'd ever done. It gave me enough money to go back to New York. And New York is where I wound up connecting with Mary J. Blige. My failures in LA gave me the drive to spin that forward and make that happen.

The reality is that the rejection in LA was actually working in my favor; it was the pull of my dream that brought me back to New York City, back to Uptown Records, Bad Boy Records, Mary, Puffy, Missy. I was *meant* to be there, at the beginning of that energy. They were the musicians and artists of that era, and I was the choreographer, the dancer, the collaborator.

My failure to become a Fly Girl and to gain traction in LA was actually something *great*. It's what eventually put me in the exact spot, when I was working on Mary J. Blige's second album, to say, "Mare, I have an idea." That led to me becoming her dance captain—I was too afraid to call myself a choreographer at first, because choreographers had better know what they were talking about. But I *was* a choreographer, and God showed me that very quickly.

I was stepping into purpose.

In fact, God showed me more than that. In order to pull off the choreography I envisioned, we needed to build a set of stairs for the show. And since there wasn't anybody else to do it, I went ahead and designed what those stairs should look like, and where they should go, and how they should move. I *directed* that, even though I wasn't a director.

I was now operating from a different inspiration, and it *worked*. Mary was like, "Wow! Yes. You have to do this."

Another step. All because Mary trusted me to try out my ideas.

I had no idea that I had that visionary gift, or that it was separate from my role as a dancer or choreographer, until I had to make a choice. I realized that I couldn't dance and choreograph and get out all of these things that were inside my head at the same time.

That was traumatizing for me. How could I fail to dance with Mary J. Blige? How could I fail to be a dancer in my own vision?

Deciding not to dance on that tour and to focus instead on direction and choreography was probably one of the hardest things I'd ever done. But then I realized: It wasn't a *failure*. It wasn't even my choice. It was my *dream's* choice, my *gift's* choice.

I hated it at first. All these other girls were onstage, living their lives, getting ready for this tour, and I was on the sidelines, *counting*.

The *bigger* wasn't there yet. I didn't know I could be a creative director or work in artist development or serve as a visionary who would design whole sets and direct videos and create the looks and feels of entire world tours. I was in between understanding.

In those moments, you have to be strong enough to trust the dream and *evolve*.

It's hard! Who wants to let go of the comfort of what people say is successful? I imagined people saying, "You're a dancer for Mary J. Blige! Why would you wanna stop that to just 'choreograph'? What's *that*?" I was in the hip-hop world. People didn't know choreographers or the extent of the type of visionaries they were. At the time it just looked like I was failing because I wasn't onstage.

I'm sad even thinking about those feelings. It was terrible. It was isolating. If only I could've seen back then what God had in store for me. I wouldn't have felt sad at all!

I'm thankful I trusted the feeling of the dream, though, because I couldn't shake those visions. When I heard Mary's music, in my mind I saw the dancers exit stage left and stage right. I needed army coats and I needed swords, and then the stairs—the stairs would be the front of her stoop in Queens. "Everybody to the stoop!" Then the stairs would turn into the bedroom. Now we're using them to descend from heaven. That staircase turned into nine million different things, and Mary was so amazing because she trusted everything. She would *run* to the stairs like it was everything I told her it was. And her dancers were all hip-hop dancers, pure raw talent. I was the only technically trained person in the bunch, so I had every freedom to use my passion to paint and create, and it was *so* good.

But there was just too much to do, and I realized I couldn't gain the respect of my dancers if I put on an outfit and went onstage with them. It was devastating.

I didn't know I was stepping into purpose.

While I was in the process of becoming, I just had to choose my yes—my new yes—and trust it.

That is not easy. Maybe you've already been through it. Chances are, if you have and you're still on your path, it'll happen to you again at some point.

As uncomfortable as it is, when the gift pushes you out of the nest, you *fly*. You're just flying a different way. And it's a tug-of-war, because something is right about that old part of the dream too. But if you're evolving, you have to know when it's time to let that part go.

I would come to realize that I could *always* dance. But if I wanted to lean in to this *new* yes, I had to let some of that old feeling go.

That was hard! I was riveted with sadness. My *dream* was to dance! How could I let go of that for *this*?

My world was swirling.

Mary's show was a *hit* because it looked like a Broadway production. I remember Puffy standing next to me at one of the shows and saying something like, "Wow, this show is amazing. Who *are* you?" He knew who I was, obviously, but it was in that moment that he realized, *Something's* on *with this one*. He knew that early that I was special.

Because I took on Mary's choreography, I was given the opportunity to choreograph for a new artist who was in a girl group called Sista. The artist was Missy "Misdemeanor" Elliott, and she was going solo. People from Missy's record company—primarily Sylvia Rhone, the first female CEO in the history of the music industry, who is just a genius woman—found out that I was doing Mary's show. When they gave me the opportunity to choreograph Missy's video for "I Can't Stand the Rain," I finally realized what had happened: "Oh, wow. I did that video. I wasn't just *in* it; I put that whole *zhoosh* together. Wow! Okay, so I'm a choreographer and director and creative visionary. Now I have to evolve this part of my gift!"

I was stepping into my purpose, God's purpose, just by saying yes. It was the start of the journey that would eventually lead me to the Monster Ball Tour for Gaga, where I did everything: the stairs, the sets, the costumes, the choreography, the full scope of everything an artistic director and creative visionary could do on one tour.

Stepping into purpose led me to grow. It brought me more and more success. Falling down and adjusting and growing and changing gave me the boom-*kack*-ability to develop a unique vision for every artist I ever worked with instead of sticking to one idea and trying to adapt it to the artists as they came along.

Stepping into purpose allowed me to evolve and to flow and to work with all types of artists. Because it wasn't about *me*; it was about my gift. It was about God and *his* vision for me. My life became all about having the ability to help others tap into their gifts and express them through dance, through staging, through a look, through an attitude change, through the mediums of television and videos. Sometimes that inspiration even carried over into artists' lyrics or the choices they made for their albums, or it gave a little kick to the power of the sound that they brought into the studio—because inspiration begets inspiration, and when creative people who are in touch with God's gifts work together, the power of those gifts tends to multiply in exponential ways.

The artists I work with inspire me too! The big ones you know by name and the ones that you might never hear of. The creativity is what matters. Staying in touch with the gift is what matters. Seeing the gifts in each of us is something we can all pay more attention to.

Each of my artists has their own world, and it's important that we not only inspire people but *free* people to create their worlds—worlds that come from the inside out; that come from their dreams; that come from God.

Just as I inspired those artists, I want to inspire you and free you to create your own world too. To overcome Dreamkillers and step into your purpose.

If you're encountering Dreamkillers, it's because you have a God-given capacity to be *more*. I've said this before and I'll say it again: the more capacity you have, the more Dreamkillers show up. But if you change your perspective, you'll realize that they're there to force you into your fullest self. Pressure makes diamonds, right? In our world, pressure is the opposition, the doubters and naysayers. That pressure creates the grinding that brings out your real *shine*. When you understand that as a part of your journey, you're able to move through and around Dreamkillers with more ease than ever—because you know they're a sign that you're headed for a better place.

That applies even when the naysayer in question is *you*.

Get Up and Dance!

Alicia Keys was clearly an incredibly gifted, talented young woman. But when I met her, she was terrified to stand up and walk away from the piano when she performed. Behind the keyboard, where she played and sang, she was in her comfort zone. But to get her to stand up in front of the microphone and sing without that piano was a *challenge*. And *forget* about dancing. She had convinced herself that she *couldn't* dance—because

In our world, pressure is the *opposition*, the doubters and naysayers. That pressure creates the grinding that brings out your real *shine*.

of the perception of what other people told her dance should look like.

She had to get *rid* of that.

For years I worked as her choreographer and creative director, and my biggest challenge, from the very beginning, was to get her over the idea that she couldn't do it. To get her to stop being her own naysayer. She didn't *want* to dance, she said. And I had to convince her that what she didn't want was to dance some *other* person's dance.

We *all* need to get over that perception. The dance we need to dance is our own.

It started with the simple act of standing up. Alicia had a hard time leaving the piano to walk to the microphone. She didn't know when to do it or how to recognize when there was a break in the music that would make that walk worthwhile and powerful; she was afraid she'd look awkward when she walked; she felt naked just standing there without a baby grand in front of her body.

I was like, "Okay, girl, you *have* to leave the piano and you *have* to trust your version of the dance, your version of the song—the *physical experience* of the song. When people buy a ticket, they don't buy a ticket to see you held hostage behind an instrument. We want to do this for them, for your audience. But also I just want you to know that there's *freedom* in letting go, in going to the middle of the stage and letting loose!"

I taught her that freedom one step at a time. I helped her find what I call "the empty" in the music, the perfect spot to stand up and let go, to let herself be free to just *sing* and not play and not have the energy of her body blocked by anything.

Then I tried to get her to sway and move and step, but she was so grounded in keeping her feet on the floor, I laughed. "You're Lead-Foot Louie!" I said.

"See, I told you!" she replied.

"I got it. Okay, Allie. You know what? We're gonna work with that. We gonna *stay* in the ground. We gonna figure out how to make that *hot*!"

What I had to convince her is that I didn't want her to "dance." I just wanted her to move like *her*, and we would turn that into her *style*.

She was down with that. So we started working—and she started *moving*.

She wasn't Beyoncé. She wasn't Britney Spears. She wasn't Madonna. She was *Alicia Keys*. Her language was molasses. She moved *slow*, and it was beautiful! And by moving exactly the way a freed-up Alicia Keys could move, she wound up *dancing*, moving her body, walking, getting up from the instrument that gave her so much comfort. By the end, she was on top of the piano, on her knees, throwing her hair back and forth!

Once she trusted that she didn't have to dance like anyone else, we were able to put together a whole dance routine for her—with *canes*. For her Grammy performance with Joaquin Phoenix, she did a whole *tango*. I was like, "Girl, you're *dancing*." This brilliant, unapologetic, soulful artist, who never wanted to leave the piano, was able to live out a performance designed for *her*.

Alicia Keys won eight Grammys on my watch, and obviously all kinds of things after that too. She gave me her platinum-album award for "Songs in A Minor." It's hanging in my house, with a picture of her at the piano. Learning to dance her dance was one of Alicia's final steps in stepping into her purpose as a world changer, a global superstar, onstage in front of hundreds of thousands of people.

There's a lesson in that. For everyone.

There's so much excellence in who Alicia is that if she does it *her* way, you feel the purity, the soulfulness, the authenticity in her movement. She doesn't have to do what somebody else has to do, because she's powerful when she simply raises her hand. That's the dance for her. At times, the dance for all of us is that simple.

Some people have to do thirty-two counts of eight; some people only have to do one. Once you know which one you are, all you have to do is *do it*. If you express that one thing truly— truly from the center of *you*—it will resonate. People will get it.

As a painter, you might have the capacity to put everything into one color. Or maybe you need lots of colors, and all the craziness of a Jackson Pollock, to connect.

It all comes down to knowing yourself and your capacity. If you don't know it yet, then it's about trusting your gift and your dream along the journey to find it and fulfill it. And when you know that you've found your utopia, you become *electric* at it. You don't add to it, force it, try to explain it. You just allow it to be. When you feel the need to press on and gain more knowledge to fulfill *more* capacity, then you keep moving.

By allowing yourself to grow and risk; by getting up in front of that microphone and allowing yourself to overcome your fear; by not judging your success by someone else's version of the dance or someone else's version of success or someone else's road but instead by learning to appreciate that you are stepping into purpose—you wind up honoring *yourself*.

I know because it happened to me.

My dream to dance was actually a dream to *inspire*. That's what I've been so blessed to be able to do.

And now? *You* have these words, *you* have this experience, *you* have me saying to you, "Five, six, seven, eight—get up!"

Everything you need is already within you. The dream is there, and all you have to do is to hang on to the dream, like I did.

How did a little girl from Toronto with nothing but a dream get to work with and inspire and be inspired by so many amazing artists? How is it possible that through my own gift—and through the collaborative sharing of our connected gifts—I've been blessed to be able to inspire millions of people with the music and the dances and the stories of all those artists? How have I been a part of moments and memories that last lifetimes and may well inspire connections across *generations*?

How does that *happen*?

It all came from my God-given dream.

It's not over. Not even close. If you ask me, I'm just getting started. And *you're* just getting started. Everything we've experienced so far is just a warm-up for what comes next. My dream continues to grow—just as *your* dream will continue to grow—as you *live it*.

STEP 8

Live Your Dream

*Y*our dream is real. It is who you are.

As time and experience add up, as your faith in your dream grows deeper, there will come a point when you're going to transform. You'll go from *becoming* to actually *being* the gift. You'll be the version of yourself you were meant to be.

God wants us to get to a place where we are unapologetically in the space of *being*. In that space, no matter what comes against us, we make our choices from a place of being the dancer, being the musician, being the painter, being the architect, being the performer, being the superstar, being the athlete, being the entrepreneur, being the visionary, being that which is expressed in your dream. To "be" means that is where you wake up from and where you operate from. It doesn't happen when society at large or some higher-up human gives you a title and tells you that you've arrived. It happens when you *know* your dream, your truth, because you live it every day, unmeasured by anything outside of yourself and your love and your passion for God's gift in *you*.

How do you get there?

You set your alarm clock to remind yourself to move toward the goal: "Dreamer, wake up today and choose to believe in the next step."

Three weeks from now: "Good morning, dreamer. Now that you've taken two steps toward your dream, take two more."

Check in with yourself: "Dreamer, where are you this morning? What will you do today to chase your dream, to express your truth, to stay in touch with your passion and all you have to give?"

There's as much power in talking to ourselves as in talking to God. Really, talking to ourselves *is* talking to God, because he created us and is one with us. Jesus explained, "I am in My Father, and you in Me, and I in you" (John 14:20).

The Bible also reminds us, "Lean not on your own understanding" (Proverbs 3:5). God is too big, too unfathomable, for us to understand. He gives us our dreams and our goals so that we can know him better.

Before I developed a personal relationship with God, he gave me the ability to talk to him by saying to myself, "Laurieann, come on. Get up! You can do this!"

And time after time, just by telling myself that I *could*—I *did*.

I dared to dream, I empowered the purpose, I trained and sustained, I stayed in my yes, I danced my truth, I found my team, I stepped into purpose—and that allowed me to *live* my dream.

Now, when certain people in the world want to tell me, "You're too old now; you can't do this," I dig down and say, "Okay, but what does *God* tell me?" And what God tells me, through the feeling of my dream, is that I'm not finished.

I don't have my big house in the hills yet. I don't have X amount of money in the bank yet. (But by faith, I do!) So I've got to keep going because that is the promise of God. I still feel the hunger. I know I have more capacity.

Today that capacity is being filled by my work with artists of all styles, of all backgrounds, at all levels—from beginners to superstars. My capacity is being filled in ways I never would have expected based on my past. But God knew more than I did.

I never would have imagined that in 2020 I would be called

to serve as an executive producer on a reboot of *Making the Band*—the show that first made me a public figure, the show that gave me such angst and worry, the show that broke my heart. Only this time, in this season, when I've learned to be the person I was always meant to be, I'm not serving as talent on-screen at the whims of others; I'm helping to *choose* the talent, to design the show, to set the tone, to bring my truth as I launch a new band and a whole new brand alongside Puff Daddy and the crew at MTV.

I'm calling the shots of my own life, my own career. To put it a different way: I'm in alignment with what God wants for my life. I'm following the dream and the glorious plan that God laid out for me, as my choreographer and creative director. It's been a long journey to get here. A long journey of *becoming* in order to finally *be*.

Don't buy into the titles of the Dreamkillers and the naysayers who want to keep you down or keep you in your box. Instead, buy into what *I'm* saying. Buy into *you*.

Everybody has their own spotlight. And that spotlight has nothing to do with an organized rollout from a PR company and everything to do with real life. Not a series, not a moment, not fifteen minutes of fame, but *real life*. Man's interpretation of that spotlight is found in the entertainment business: "Catch me on *So You Think You Can Dance*, guys! Watch me on *Making the Band*!" But I'm talking about a success that is not measured by man's limited perception of value.

Yes, I'm on TV, and I'll be on TV more in the future. When you tune in, tune in to have fun with me. TV is for enjoyment. But then? Turn it off and focus on becoming the best version of *yourself*. Go live under your *own* spotlight.

I'm in *alignment* with what God wants for my life. I'm following the *dream* and the glorious *plan* that God laid out for me, as my *choreographer* and creative director.

Enjoy me when I'm dancing; enjoy the singers you see when they're singing. But don't feel as though you're less than because your journey hasn't taken you there yet. This is entertainment. You're not supposed to compare yourself to the imagery, and you're definitely not supposed to feel like you're a nobody. You're supposed to be entertained, and then wake up the next morning and live *your* best life on the way to becoming your best state of being.

One of the most important ways to do that is to be grateful for what you *have*.

As you start to live your dream, as you move from becoming to being, you'll find that gratitude is a way of life. It is a verb.

It's not just for the big moments; it's *every* moment. It's the attitude that keeps you humble, because you're grateful for the gifts that unfold right in front of you.

Once you're willing to put yourself in alignment with what God wants for you, to live and breathe your dream in everything you do, you tap into your God-given greatness. In your greatness, you can access *the flow*, the feeling that happens when life is just clicking for you. If you stay in tune with it, you can ride that flow as far as you want to.

Other people will see the power of what's unfolding in your life, and some might try to dismiss it as "luck" or something else that's far less than what it actually is. But you'll know it's the expression of the abundant blessing that God wants for all of us. How can you not be grateful for that?

When you're in the flow, you see that life's ups and downs are really not difficult, because you trust in your dream and in the process. You live in a state of gratefulness because you no longer second-guess who you ultimately will be, and you cannot be compared to anybody else.

When you fall into that flow, when you fall into that state of grace, *that* is when you move from *becoming* to *being*.

That's where I am today. Just being me.

I am living out new rewards for that. And I am so grateful for those rewards and for the people who believed in me even when nobody else did. By no coincidence, it seems many of them are moving from becoming to being too. And we're finally sharing in that being, *together*.

A Seat at The Table

A couple of weeks before the 2020 Grammys, I got a call.

Puff Daddy was going to be the recipient of an Icon Award, which would be celebrated at a pre-Grammy party the night before the big show. Let me clarify: not just any pre-Grammy party; the Clive Davis Pre-Grammy Gala. The biggest party in town. The impossible ticket to get. One of the most celebrated, anticipated, coveted annual parties in the entire music business.

The organizers asked me to curate a performance full of artists to celebrate Puffy's career.

To be invited to be a part of the Clive Davis Pre-Grammy Gala is a high achievement; it's the benchmark for knowing when you've made it in the music industry.

I could not have been more honored. At least, I *thought* I could not have been more honored.

I had a twenty-minute slot to put on a show honoring my longtime friend and mentor, this man who was family to me—and I wanted it to be *spectacular*. The kind of thing where each performer who came out would be a surprise to him and to the whole audience of music-industry insiders and superstars. So I started working the phones, pulling every string I had.

It turns out, after all these years and all this hard work *becoming*, I had a lot of strings to pull. More than I even realized.

It didn't matter to me that I'd be standing on the side stage watching the tribute unfold, and not in the audience or on the stage. I didn't need any of that. I was grateful just to be there, to be me, giving Puffy the honor of a lifetime through what I would create, envision, assemble, choreograph, direct, and produce.

But then, a few nights before the party, Puff sent me a message that ended with ". . . Oh, and you're sitting at my table."

It wasn't anything I asked for or expected—but I got a little emotional when I read those words. People like me, the choreographers and creative directors, rarely get to sit in the room when the show's happening. We certainly don't get a seat at the table with the honoree and his closest confidants. That's a spot for the head of the record label and other superstars, right?

I can't believe it, I thought. *I finally got a seat at the table.*

God had always promised me that. Now here it was—a physical representation to say, "I made it." Not in *their* way, but in *my* way. In *God's* way. It was a long road, but it was the *right* road for me.

So I sat there that night, surrounded by people like Jay-Z and Beyoncé, and Cyndi Lauper (who got up and sang "Girls Just Want to Have Fun" and blew the whole room away), and Janet Jackson, who stayed quietly in the back, and all sorts of A&R guys and lawyers I'd worked with, and all kinds of familiar faces from the industry I'd been so fortunate to be a part of for so long—including a few sharks who I swear were trying to steal my money! I sat at Puff's table, right next to the incredible executive and pioneer Sylvia Rhone, as the tribute show I put together began.

Puff's had so many hits that there was no way to reference them all in twenty minutes. So I approached every choice with intention. I wanted the show to be an emotional ride about his passion for the music and how that makes you feel.

I started off with Faith Evans. "Soon as I Get Home" is a big R&B song, and she can sing her face off. So I wanted the room to be clear about the fact that Sean knows real music, real voices, real R&B. I didn't want to come in with the party energy right away, so I started with Faith, and she blew the room away. Then we transitioned into Carl Thomas, another incredible vocalist, and then to Mase and Lil' Kim, so we got to the rap energy and the party. Then I closed with something *nobody* saw coming: Puff's son Christian singing "Missing You." Christian's like twenty-one now, and he's the spitting image of his dad at that age. Christian had lost his mom, Puff's baby mama Kim Porter, to pneumonia a year before this event. So it was *emotional*. Puff was crying. We all had tears in our eyes.

This moment was a long time coming, and I was just so grateful for the opportunity to pay this man a tribute in this way, through my own gift of what I had to give.

But then, something completely unexpected happened. Puff got up onstage to give a speech, and he turned the spotlight on *me*. For two full minutes he talked about my career, and where I'd been and what I'd done, and how I'd been both a muse and an inspiration to him. He called me a "creative genius."

I was shaking.

Sylvia was like, "Stand up. Stand up!"

But I didn't want to stand, because I felt like this wasn't

something that man could have done. This was absolutely something that God was doing. I didn't want to receive it in a personal way, a selfish way. I didn't feel like Puff was speaking to me; he was speaking to who I am, who I'd *become*, which was God's gift. It wasn't about *me*. Standing didn't feel in alignment with walking the walk.

I didn't need the spotlight. I didn't need the applause. Maybe that's why, in the moment it happened, it felt so *great*. Truly great, in the big sense of the word. It was a confirmation. I wouldn't have been in that room if I had not followed the steps in order to live my dream. It was a moment of living proof that the way I had chosen to live my life *worked*.

Beyoncé and Jay-Z and all my comrades took a moment to look my way and applaud—not for me but for my gift. *Wow.*

I looked around at the people in that room, at everyone I'd worked with and fought with and overcome with and bounced off of and supported and inspired and been inspired by. At the ones I'd been scared of or worried about or intimidated by in this constant battle of walking my own walk, my own way, to get to this place in my life and career, against so many odds. I just sat there in *awe* at what God had done.

He had proven to me that no matter what comes, you can prevail, you can *be*, as long as you dance your dance.

Looking Back

I sometimes wish I had come to my state of being sooner. I sometimes wish some of my journey could have been easier. But I know now, as I write these words, that it's unfolding exactly as it was supposed to unfold—primarily so I can share all the struggles and challenges of this journey with *you* in this book. Right here, right now.

Maybe, just maybe, you'll give the option of *becoming* a try. Because you know what? Life isn't supposed to feel bad. Life isn't supposed to always feel like a constant fight. Those times when it's *not* a fight—and I know you've had them—*that's* when you're actually feeling what you're supposed to be pursuing! That's when you're in the area you're supposed to be moving toward.

It doesn't matter *when* you realize it, only that you do.

I know the collective mindset says, "Oh, if you're not here by now, you've not done well." "If you're not here by now, you've not become what you're meant to become." That mindset is dangerous, and that mindset is sad, because how does one person know what another is capable of doing? They didn't create that person; therefore they cannot know in totality what's in that person's heart and mind.

It's time to change that mindset, to value where you are today. I want to inspire you to think a *different* way. I want to let you know that it's okay to change—*right now.*

Just because you've gone in what somebody tells you is the wrong direction for a little while—even if it's a *long* while— that doesn't mean you can't change now. Plus, what is a "wrong direction," anyway? It's just the flag to let you know what's not serving you. So rather than thinking, *I've done wrong,* you can think, *Hey, look! This road isn't the one I'm supposed to be on. That dance isn't the one I'm supposed to be dancing.*

Which might leave you asking, "Okay, then what am I supposed to be doing?"

It's okay if you don't know the answer right now. You'll begin

No matter what comes, you can *prevail*, you can *be*, as long as you *dance your dance*.

to find it simply by acknowledging, *This isn't it. This isn't my truth.* I know it's kind of scary, because that attitude calls for you to take steps without having any confirmation of sight. You have to take these steps by faith.

But no matter where you are on your faith journey, be thankful—*grateful*—that you have the chance to take those steps. You're alive! Make the most of it.

If my story has taught you anything, it's to persevere.

It's *okay* to be vulnerable and admit that you don't have all the answers; that you don't know where you're headed; that you're so far removed from your original dream that you're not even sure what your dream might have been. All of us are struggling and trying and doing the best we can. Sometimes being vulnerable is the only way to get the help we need—from other people, as well as from God.

Your career might not be in entertainment, but there is creativity in *everything.* There's creativity when a doctor goes to do open-heart surgery. In fact, you'd better hope that your doctor is creative, and in touch with their own truth, to deal with your particular heart. No matter how much they studied, once your doctor opens you up, they might find a different beat going on in there. A heart is an original thing, you know. So if your doctor is not creative in that moment, they might not have what it takes to fix you.

Your creativity is no different from Biggie's or Michael's or Gaga's or Alicia's. It's certainly no less valuable, no less worthy of our praise and admiration and awe.

You should not feel devalued by the fact that you are working at Starbucks, and every day you get your customers' coffees right, and they feel ready to go tackle their own dreams because of the coffee you and your team made. That means you have your hand on a decision that will affect the *world*. Thank God you're happy about what you do, and be grateful for that.

God's grace is a powerful thing. It's gratitude personified. It's the reason we can experience heaven on earth.

When you're in touch with that, there is no greater feeling. It's an amazing thing to strive for as you become the *you* you're meant to be. When you're experiencing heaven on earth, what's outside—the worldly possessions and manifestations of man's idea of wealth and power—becomes only a desperate attempt to decorate the greatness that continues to evolve inside you.

If only it was easier to hold on to the moments when we get a flash of the bigness of our dreams. Sometimes when we get little spurts, little bread crumbs, it's hard to remember and recognize that the dream is real. But your passion tells you it's real. It's the fire, the burn, the excitement, the joy that tells you your dream is possible. We have to trust that. We have to trust that feeling and that alignment.

It's hard to sustain. Sometimes when things are going well, you get scared that the other shoe's gonna drop. You get scared because you think your muscle isn't strong enough to sustain the moment.

Keep going. Don't worry. Be grateful you had that moment at all! The inability to sustain it is only temporary. The more you move forward in your process, the more you'll develop the right muscles to dance your dance.

I want to encourage you to stand in your spotlight, and to know that no one person's spotlight is better than another's. If you think your spotlight should be bigger than it is; if you feel the hunger, if you have the capacity; if you feel like you've been overlooked and wonder when it will be your time—please know: it's *always* your time.

In the eyes of God, if you're in touch with your dream—his dream for you—then you are already in your spotlight.

Your spotlight is *beautiful*. Undeniable. Unbreakable. Undimmable.

It's pure. And it's real.

Stand in it. It's *yours*.

Seeing The Light

Everyone has a spotlight—a spark, a dream—and when you're in touch with your own, you can't help but see it in others.

The night of the Clive Davis party, when I was on my way to work with and sit in the company of some of the biggest superstars on the planet, I happened to walk by a girl with a dog, sitting on the sidewalk in front of my local Starbucks.

She might have been homeless or not. She might have been down on her luck or not. She wasn't bothering anybody; she wasn't calling any attention to herself at all. But I saw a spotlight in her, in that particular moment, and it shined so brightly I simply could not pass her by without a word.

"Sis, you need something?" I asked.

She looked at me, eye to eye, with the connection that lets you know that no one else had made eye contact with her in a very long time. She smiled a little bit and said, "Yeah, could you get me a coffee?"

"No problem," I replied.

My authentic self was making sure that I responded to the call of buying a coffee for that girl on my way to the biggest party in the music world. I made sure I didn't miss that beat. I don't know who that girl will become, but I saw her spotlight in that moment. I brought her a coffee because I was like, *I'm bringing the superstar the coffee.* I didn't want to miss that moment to honor the clarity of seeing her light, and to let her know that she could feel valued and served—not because she had a number-one record, not because she had something to give to me, but because she was one of God's children and there is a dream in her just like there was a dream in me.

Because I've experienced God's grace, I have the responsibility to walk the walk: to believe that everyone has their spotlight, everyone has their gift, everyone has the opportunity to live the fullest version of themselves. I want to be a party to that expression in the world.

It's easy to look at a girl like that, at someone who might be homeless or a drug user, and condemn. It's easy to ignore, to turn a blind eye, even though you do not know her circumstances. What's more fulfilling? What's more beautiful? What feels better? To see this person as her best self; to see the dream that God gave her, which for whatever reason she may have denied in herself for too long.

On that incredible day, I was grateful for the gift of being able to see that girl's spotlight. To meet her right where she was, and to let her know that she could be gifted, she could be served, she could be seen. I had no agenda, no need for her to reciprocate. I only wanted to give a little acknowledgment that God is good and the world isn't as awful as she might think it is.

There *is* another way. There *is* another option. Sometimes all it takes to remind someone of that is buying them a cup of coffee.

I have tears in my eyes when I think about that moment. I

get emotional because I think that there is so much value in the power of seeing people for who they are; so much value in seeing others being themselves, being vulnerable, being real. It is one of the greatest gifts that we have. Yet we ignore it.

I believe that the spirit of love and peace should be more powerful, more prevalent, and more exposed to the masses than the ideas of the oppressors are. I get emotional because I think that what some people are "inspiring" others with is often lacking truth, lacking the *real* inspiration it takes to hold on to your dream, lacking the clarity of God's gifts, and lacking the ability to provide you with provision for your vision.

Provision is not just financial gain in order to start a business or pursue a career; provision is the inspiration and the knowledge of what unlocks the clarity in you so you can sustain and persevere and eventually *become*.

So that's why I cry—because the world so often denies people access to what it *really* takes to make it. They tell you to do things that actually tip you further away from unlocking what's limitless in *you*. Those who project greed and envy and all those things that are in opposition to truth are working *against* everything I was given the gift of working *with*.

I cry because I want people to know that a dream-based life is an option. What you've read in this book and seen in my life is an option. When you're drawn to a new option, that means that you're ready for change; that means you're ready to evolve; that means you're thirsting for what's real.

Seeing other people as they are; acknowledging that everyone is on their own journey, and that no matter where they are on that journey, they're a superstar in God's spotlight—that's a dream we *all* should share.

But in order to see it, you have to see it in yourself first; you have to hold on to your dream. When you're in that place and you feel that joy, then and only then will you see the light all around you. And what a beautiful thing that is.

When you acknowledge the light in others, you begin a new collaboration. When you see the light—in your children, in your colleagues, in people on the street—you can't help but to have the grace to acknowledge and celebrate our differences *together*.

So I beg of you, keep trying. Dig down deep, all the way back to the beginnings of your dream, and let that dream be your guide in all things.

Take these steps. Embrace them. Use them to dance *your* dance, and then share what you've learned with the people in your life to help them dance their dances too.

As more of us take the option to live our lives according to the feeling of the dream that God gave us, more of us will rise.

And that is the greatest collaboration, the greatest performance of all—the great dance to which we *all* belong.

As I said in the beginning, this is *our* dance.

So get ready.

Can you feel it?

The curtain is rising.

Acknowledgments

A special thank-you to Mark Dagostino: Thanks for believing in my story and in this book. You are a remarkable writer, and I'm very grateful to have learned from the best.

Cheryl Fox, thank you for the cover photo. Your eye catches the intention so effortlessly.

Thank you to the Haus of Boomkack for the cover art contribution, Juan Tamez (makeup) and Brandon Green (stylist).

Thank you to Mitchell Solarek and Dennis Disney and everyone at Maximum Artist Management. Mitchell, thank you for believing in all things Boomkack! You're undeniably the best. Dennis, thank you for covering me and directing me and taking all the late-night, last-minute phone calls. Your expertise is unmatched.

I would like to thank HarperCollins Christian Publishing for the opportunity, and the entire team for being a part of my first book. Shout-out to Meaghan Porter for seeing the vision.

Finally, last but not least, to Joshua Gibson-Bascombe, nephew and CEO of Bkww: This book would have not existed without your persistence. Thank you for drafting the book outline to get this deal. In addition, thank you to my family for always supporting me and being there for me throughout this incredible journey.

About The Authors

Laurieann Gibson is one of the most important pop-culture influencers in entertainment today. Having served as director and choreographer for numerous international superstars such as Katy Perry, Lady Gaga, Diddy, and Alicia Keys, Gibson brings a unique brand of blending traditional artist development with movement and dance training to their collaborations. A classically trained dancer, Gibson studied at the prestigious Alvin Ailey Dance Company, segueing from traditional theater dance to hip-hop with breakout artist Mary J. Blige. Over the years, Gibson's expertise in developing artists' performance skills along with her choreography and creative insight has led to her choreographing and directing world tours for some of today's biggest pop acts, as well as numerous television appearances, including as a judge on *So You Think You Can Dance* and the return of *Making the Band*. She lives in Los Angeles, California, with her doggie "son," Samson.

Mark Dagostino is a multiple *New York Times* bestselling coauthor who is dedicated to writing books that uplift and inspire. Prior to writing books, he spent ten years on staff in New York and Los Angeles as a correspondent, columnist, and senior writer for *People* magazine. He now lives a somewhat quieter life in New Hampshire.